GROUNDWORK GUIDES

Series Editor
Jane Springer

GROUNDWORK GUIDES

Slavery Today
Kevin Bales &
Becky Cornell

Groundwood Books
House of Anansi Press

Toronto Berkeley

Groundwood Books / House of Anansi Press
110 Spadina Avenue, Suite 801, Toronto, Ontario M5V 2K4
or c/o Publishers Group West
1700 Fourth Street, Berkeley, CA 94710

We acknowledge for their financial support of our publishing
program the Canada Council for the Arts, the Government of Canada
through the Book Publishing Industry Development Program (BPIDP)
and the Ontario Arts Council.

ONTARIO ARTS COUNCIL
CONSEIL DES ARTS DE L'ONTARIO

Library and Archives Canada Cataloguing in Publication
Bales, Kevin
Slavery today / Kevin Bales and Becky Cornell.
(Groundwork guides)
Includes index.
ISBN-13: 978-0-88899-772-2 (bound).
ISBN-10: 0-88899-772-8 (bound).
ISBN-13: 978-0-88899-773-9 (pbk.)
ISBN-10: 0-88899-773-6 (pbk.)
1. Slavery. 2. Slave labor. I. Title. II. Series.
HT867.B35 2008   306.3'62   C2008-900525-2

Design by Michael Solomon
Printed and bound in Canada

This book is printed on paper that contains 100% post-consumer
recycled fibers, is acid-free and is processed chlorine-free.

Contents

Chapter 1
The New Slavery

Although many people think slavery is a thing of the past, it exists all around us. In the rich countries of the world, slaves suffer as servants, agricultural workers and prostitutes. In the developing world, slaves cultivate and harvest food, and work in small factories, the fishing industry and thousands of other jobs. Some of the commodities and goods they produce flow through the global market into our homes. Each year slavery generates billions of dollars for criminals who prey on the most vulnerable — the poor, the uneducated and the impoverished immigrant seeking a better life. Those working to free slaves around the world are few in number and under-resourced. Most slaves today have little chance of liberation. Those who do survive enslavement face enormous challenges as they struggle to regain control of their shattered lives.

No one knows exactly how many slaves there are in the world. Slavery is illegal in virtually every country, which means it is hidden from view. But a careful review of all the information available suggests that there are about 27 million slaves alive today. The biggest part of that 27 million, perhaps 15 to 20 million, is in South Asia: India, Pakistan and Nepal. Slavery is also concentrated in Southeast Asia, in Northern and Western Africa, and in parts of South America. However, there are some slaves in almost every country in the world, including the United States, Canada, Japan and most European countries. To put it in perspective, today's slave population is greater than the population of Australia and almost seven times greater than the population of Ireland.

What Makes a Slave?

Most of us have a picture of slavery in our minds drawn from history. It may be the slaves of the Southern US before the Civil War, or the slaves of ancient Egypt. Many people think slavery is about owning people, but the key to slavery is not about ownership but about how people are controlled. Since the beginning of history, the primary characteristic that has defined slavery is violence. Slaves cannot walk away, cannot make any choices about anything in their lives, because they are held under complete control that is backed up by violence. Many people who become slaves are tricked into it. Many people, following a trail of lies, walk into slavery, but what keeps them there is violence. Once enslaved, there are all sorts of ways that slaves are held in slavery — sometimes it is the way the slave gives up and gives in to slavery; sometimes it is about the personal relationships that develop between slaves and slaveholders — but if they try to escape or show resistance, then they will be hurt.

The second key characteristic of slavery is <u>loss of free will</u>. Slaves remain under the complete control of someone else, the slaveholder. There is no other person, authority or government the slave can turn to for protection. Slaves must do as they are told or they will suffer. A third characteristic of slavery is economic exploitation. Slavery is about money. People are enslaved to make a profit. Most slaveholders have little interest in hurting anyone, in being cruel or torturing someone; it is simply part of the job. In order to make the most money, slaves are not paid, just given what is needed to keep them alive, if barely.

When we put these characteristics together, we can define slavery in this way: slavery is a social and economic relationship in which a person is controlled through violence or the threat of violence, is paid nothing, and is economically exploited.

In some ways this is a narrow definition, but it is broad enough to include the many kinds of slavery that exist around the world. A definition that works for many different types of slavery is important because slavery, like all human relationships, changes over time.

The key to slavery is violent control, the fact that a person cannot walk away. This means that while other forms of exploitation, such as working in a sweatshop, may appear to be slavery, they may not be. If a person can walk away from a bad situation, then he or she is probably not in slavery. This is not to deny in any way the terrible exploitation that exists in sweatshops or unfree forms of arranged marriage, for example. There is a terrible continuum of exploitation around the world and slavery exists at the extreme end of that continuum.

Contemporary Slavery

Slavery today differs from slavery in the past in three important ways. First, slaves today are cheaper than they have ever been. The cost of slaves has fallen to a historical low, and they can be acquired in some parts of the world for as little as $10. (All dollars are US$.) Second, the length of time that slaves are held has also fallen. In the past, slavery was usually a lifelong condition; today it is often temporary, lasting just a few years or even months. Short-term slavery is dangerous because the slaveholder has less incentive to keep the slave healthy or even alive.

Third, slavery is globalized, meaning that forms of slavery in different parts of the world are becoming more alike. The way slaves are used and the part they play in the world economy are increasingly similar, wherever they are. These three changes have come about very quickly, occurring, for the most part, since the end of World War II.

The slavery that we face today has been shaped largely by a number of interrelated factors. One is the population explosion that occurred after World War II. It took all of human history for the world's population to reach about 2 billion people in 1927 — it then took only seventy-two years for that number to triple to 6 billion in 1999 (see chart on page 12). Currently, the population is about 6.5 billion and it is projected to grow to 7 billion by 2013.[1] The greatest part of the population increase has taken place in the developing world, where slavery is also the most prevalent.

Another factor supporting the growth of slavery is the rapid change in the global economy that has increased the poverty and vulnerability of large parts of the population in the developing world. Throughout Africa, Asia and much of South America, the last fifty years have been marked by civil war or wars for independence from colonial powers, and the wholesale looting of resources by leaders and elites who were often supported by the powerful nations of Europe and North America. Countries with little to sell on the world market have been put deeply into debt to pay for the weapons the leaders — often dictators — used to hold on to power. Meanwhile, traditional family farming was sacrificed to concentrate

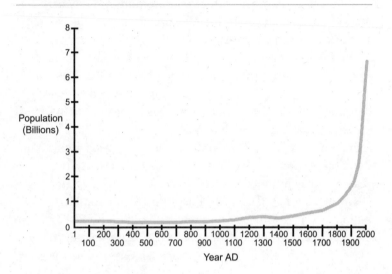

Source: Kevin Bales, Free the Slaves

on raising cash crops that could be sold to pay off those foreign debts. As the world economy grew and became more global, it had a profound impact on people in the Global South and the small-scale farming that supported many of them. The loss of common land shared by all the people in a village and government policies that pushed down the prices farmers were paid for crops to ensure cheap food for city workers have helped to bankrupt millions of peasants and drive them from their land. All across the developing world the slums and shantytowns that surround big cities hold millions of these displaced people. They come to the cities in search of jobs, but find they are competing for them with thousands of other displaced people. With little income and no job security, they are powerless and very vulnerable.

Some national and global policies also threaten these vulnerable and displaced people. The United States government pays $19 billion a year to subsidize American farmers. For example, the US gives $4 billion a year to cotton farmers to help them grow a crop that is valued at only $3 billion. The cotton farmers in India, Benin, Mali, Burkina Faso and Togo (all countries with high levels of slavery) cannot compete with this subsidy. Though they actually raise cotton at a lower cost than American farmers, the American farmers can beat them in the marketplace because they receive money from both the sale of the crop and from the US government. European countries also pump money into the pockets of their own farmers, creating an unfair advantage on the world market. When the global economy squeezes poor countries as it does with farm subsidies, the people there have fewer and fewer options. In the disruption that comes with rapid social change, slavery can become one of the remaining options.

Government corruption also supports slavery. Just having lots of vulnerable people doesn't automatically make them slaves. To turn vulnerable people into slaves you have to use violence. In many countries, in order to use violence without being arrested, you need to pay off the police. One of the basic ideas about democracy is that the government should have a monopoly on violence.

The military and the police are generally the only ones who can legally use weapons and commit violence. But if certain individuals can use violence however and whenever they like, without fear of being arrested and locked up, they can force people into slavery. To do that with regularity requires government corruption, especially police corruption. In some countries the corruption runs so deep that the police act as slave catchers, pursuing and punishing escaped slaves. Often police make slaveholders pay bribes for "protection." For slaveholders making a profit from slaves, these bribes are just a normal part of their business. When laws against kidnapping, trafficking and slavery are not enforced, those who have the means of violence (often the police themselves) can bring in slaves.

These three broad factors — population growth, economic change and corruption — come together today to create a kind of slavery that has not been seen before in history, where slaves are cheap and disposable. But the precise causes of this phenomenon vary from country to country. Slavery grows quickly when the rule of law breaks down. Conflict and disaster open the door to criminals who use violence and trickery to enslave people. The chaos that brings slavery can have a number of causes: war and civil conflict; environmental disaster; or the slower, less dramatic but equally deadly impact of international policies that break down a poor country's ability to care for its citizens.

When war starts, slavery quickly follows. In Burma (Myanmar), the military dictatorship has been waging a war against ethnic groups within the country for many years. Enslavement into forced labor has been a regular feature of that war and many other wars as well. The way that war generates slavery was very clearly shown when Yugoslavia began to break up in the 1990s. Bordering Italy, Yugoslavia had been a stable and relatively prosperous country with modern health care and education systems. The end of the Cold War opened the country to outside investment and many thought it would quickly become as advanced as other Western European countries. When the country collapsed into civil war between ethnic groups, outside observers were at first disbelieving and then astounded to learn that slave markets had appeared in the destroyed towns and cities. Refugee women were easily captured and sold to slaveholders who forced them into prostitution.

Almost every war produces slavery. War slavery, and the enslavement of children as soldiers and servants, has been seen recently in Sierra Leone, Sri Lanka, Burma, Uganda and parts of Central America. As expendable and exploitable combatants, the children who survive suffer terrible physical and mental health problems as well as tremendous challenges in reintegrating into society. The civil war in Sudan that began in the 1980s and still continues, particularly in the Darfur region, has seen thousands of women and children enslaved. Even the invasion of Iraq in 2003 led to the trafficking and enslavement of foreign workers by US government contractors. In 2005, Iraqi insurgents fighting to force out the US military murdered twelve Nepali men who had been trafficked into the country to work on US bases.[2]

Slavery is also linked to environmental destruction. Around the world slaves are being used to destroy the natural environment, and in a vicious cycle, that destruction generates more and more slaves. The criminals who destroy the lives of slaves care just as little for the environment. Slaves are used to cut down the trees of the Amazon rain forest and the mountain forests of Burma. Slaves work in open pit mines digging for gold, diamonds and other minerals; these mines scar the landscape in Brazil, Ghana, Liberia, India and the Congo. It is easy to see this cycle of slavery and environmental destruction in India. There, dam construction forces farmers from their land without compensation. One dam currently under construction on the Narmada River will submerge 245 villages and displace 200,000 people.[3] Pushed off their land, these small farmers cannot just start farming somewhere else; the surrounding land is already taken. Soon, their only alternative becomes debt. In rural India this means slavery through debt bondage. Once in bondage, slaveholders will put them to work on land that is "available" in the national forests or other protected areas. Here they cut down the trees and dig quarries and more of the natural world is destroyed. This then displaces more farmers and the cycle begins again.

War and environmental destruction are visible and dramatic phenomena, but the slow deterioration of an economy can also bring slavery in its wake. Most slavery occurs in the poorer parts of the world and many of these countries are poor not because they lack resources, but because the citizens have lost control of their economies.

Sometimes this happens when corrupt leaders take over a country. Such leaders are called "kleptocrats," and the Burmese dictators are a good example. Perhaps the champion kleptocrat was Charles Taylor, the former dictator of Liberia. Taylor stripped nearly all the wealth from his country, selling off its hospital equipment and even the desks and light fixtures from schools. Helped by international arms dealers, he terrorized the country and thousands of people were enslaved to dig for diamonds at gunpoint. When he was finally driven from Liberia, he took $3 billion with him.

It is no coincidence that Liberia's international debt is also about $3 billion. Many of the countries with high levels of slavery suffer from "debt overhang." As economist Jeffrey Sachs explains, "Debt from the past crushes the prospects of growth in the future."[4] This means that much of the national income has to go to pay back international banks, so little money is left to help the people or even enforce the law. Dictators like Taylor take out enormous loans, the funds of which are simply stolen or used to buy weapons to oppress the people.

The relationship between international debt and slavery is very clear. Countries with large debts cannot spend money on the things that are most likely to reduce the extent of slavery — schools, law enforcement, economic growth. The table on page 18 shows the link between international debt and slavery for 204 countries. The high-debt countries are concentrated in sub-Saharan Africa and include states with a high level of slavery such as Mauritania, Ghana, Niger and the Congo. The persistent

Levels of Debt and Levels of Slavery for 204 Countries

Amount of Slavery in Country

	High-Debt Countries	All Other Countries
No Slavery	2.6%	25.3%
Very Little or Rare Slavery	5.3%	36.2%
Persistent, Low Level of Slavery	42.1%	25.9%
Slavery in Some Economic Sectors	26.3%	7.8%
Slavery in Many Economic Sectors	23.7%	4.8%
Total % (number of nations)	100% (38)	100% (166)

Source: Kevin Bales, Free the Slaves

but low level of slavery that the chart shows to exist in countries without a high debt reflects the fact that human trafficking carries slaves into the rich countries of North America and Europe.

If you add together war, environmental destruction and economic crisis, you create the two main causes of slavery: poverty and violence. Poverty makes people vulnerable and desperate, leaving them without the resources to care for themselves. Yet poverty alone is not enough. To convert the poor and vulnerable into slaves requires violence. Violence is the key to slavery and violence runs wild when the rule of law breaks down due to war, environmental crisis, or the corruption that comes with economic collapse.

The Price of Slaves

The poorest of the poor in the Global South are the 1 billion people who live on $1 a day or less. Most slaves are drawn from this pool of very poor and vulnerable people. In a dramatic example of supply and demand, there are so many potential slaves that their price has fallen and fallen. Slaves are now so cheap that they have become cost-effective in many new kinds of work. The low cost of slaves has also increased the amount of potential profit and tended to decrease the length of time a person might be enslaved. It has made the question of legal ownership less important too. When slaves were expensive, it was important to safeguard that investment by having clear and legally documented ownership. Slaves of the past were worth stealing and worth chasing down if they escaped. Today, slaves are cheap and that makes them disposable.

When a slaveholder acquires a slave, he or she is looking to obtain not only an individual, but the total productivity and labor of that individual. The ability to control another person *and* all the future labor of that person is a very valuable asset. Historically, slaveholders paid a lot for a slave and that slave's productive capacity.

Many different items have been traded for slaves, but two things were regularly traded for slaves throughout history: oxen and land. The Greek philosopher Aristotle once called the ox "a poor man's slave." An ox is similar to a slave in that when you purchase an ox you not only own the ox, but also all of the work the ox will perform for the rest of its life. In modern terms, an ox would be about equivalent to a tractor on a small farm, and a field would be generally thought of as a productive patch of land that can be tended by one person. As with the slave and the ox, when you buy a field you own both the field and everything that the field will produce in the future.

At different points in history, a slave was worth different numbers of oxen and fields. In Sumer in 2000 BC a slave was worth two oxen or one field. In Greece in 800 BC a slave was worth four oxen, and in Rome in AD 200, eight oxen. During the Middle Ages in England a slave was worth between four and eight oxen. In the United States between 1847 and 1859, a single slave was worth between four and seven oxen, or two to three fields. Following the abolition of slavery in the US, there are fewer records of the price of slaves, because slavery became illegal. The prices that are available for slaves during the twentieth century show a rapid fall in the price of slaves concurrent with the period of the population explosion.

The figure on page 21 shows how the price of slaves has fallen to an all-time low in the last fifty years. The price index in this graph uses a number of measures, including oxen and land, to calculate the value of a slave at different times in history. As a comparison, the price index score of 4 for the year 1856 would be equal to about $40,000 today. Today, slaves can be purchased for less than $100. In 2001, in the West African country of

Price of Slaves, 2000 BC to AD 2004

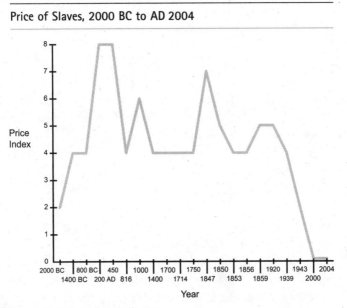

Source: Kevin Bales, Free the Slaves

Ivory Coast, a researcher purchased two nineteen-year-old agricultural workers for about $40 each.[5] The loan a slaveholder uses to enslave bonded laborers in India can be between $10 and $100 and the families may be in slavery for several generations for that price.

The fact that slaves are now disposable means that new slavery is less permanent. Slaveholders are not interested in keeping a slave who is not making a profit. Although most slaves are held for years, some are held for only a few months. In countries where sugar cane is grown, for example, people may be enslaved for a single harvest because it is not worth feeding and housing them until the next harvest. Slaves in the American South in the nineteenth century were like valuable livestock; the owner needed to make back his investment. There was also pressure to breed them and produce more slaves, since it was usually cheaper to raise new slaves than to buy adults. Today no slaveholder wants to spend money supporting useless infants. Today slaves are thrown out when they are no longer producing a profit, or when they can no longer work hard or are weak or sick.

In 1850 in the US cotton plantations, an average field laborer was selling for $1,000 to $1,200, which in today's money would equal around $40,000. If the cotton market went up, a plantation owner could make a very good profit on his slaves, but if the price of cotton fell, he might be forced to sell slaves to stay in business. There were bills of sale and titles of ownership for slaves, and slaves could be used as collateral for loans or to pay off

Differences Between Old and New Slavery

Old Forms of Slavery	New Forms of Slavery
Legal ownership asserted	Legal ownership avoided
High purchase cost	Very low purchase cost
Low profits	Very high profits
Shortage of potential slaves	Surplus of potential slaves
Long-term relationship	Short-term relationship
Slaves maintained	Slaves disposable
Ethnic differences important	Ethnic differences less important

debts. Violence was used to keep slaves under control, but too much violence could ruin a big investment. At that time, as well, slavery was directly related to race. Slavery was so racist that a very small genetic difference — being one-eighth "black" and seven-eighths "white" — could mean lifelong enslavement. Before the Civil War, many people in the United States believed "one drop of black blood" meant that you were black and therefore could be enslaved.

Now compare that with the young women enslaved in prostitution in Thailand today, where rapid economic change has led to new poverty and desperation. Young Thai women and girls are lured from rural areas with the promise of work in restaurants or factories. There is little ethnic difference between the slaves and slaveholders; if anything, the key difference is rural (slaves) versus urban (slaveholders). The slave recruiter offers the girls' parents an "advance" on their wages, but once they are away from their homes they are brutalized and enslaved and sold to a brothel. The brothel owners tell the girls they must pay back their purchase price plus interest through prostitution. This is a lie; the pimp won't let the girls go until they can no longer be sold to men, because of physical or mental breakdown, no matter how much money they earn. The brothels do have to feed the girls and keep them presentable, but if they become ill or injured, they are disposed of. In Thailand today this often happens when a girl tests positive for HIV. As a business, this kind of slavery is extremely profitable. A girl aged twelve to fifteen can be purchased for $800 to $2,000 and the costs of running a brothel and feeding the girls are relatively low, especially considering how little they are fed. The profit for the slaveholder is often as high as 800 percent a year. This kind of return can be made on a young woman for three to five years. After that, especially if she becomes ill or HIV positive, she is dumped in the street. This is the face of global slavery today.

Chapter 2
Slavery Throughout History

Slavery has been around as long as human history. It is an institution that predates legal systems, the invention of money and written records. Ancient civilizations in Mesopotamia built towns with protective walls around 6800 BC, suggesting that they went to war or that towns were raided, situations where slavery often took root. Clay drawings from around 4000 BC show slaves taken by ancient Sumerians during wartime. Records from 2100 BC show that Egyptian citizens owned slaves. The oldest recorded price of a slave is eleven silver shekels — a price paid after slavery had existed for about 2,000 years. By then, slaves were being captured, bought and sold around the ancient world and slavery had become a business.

By the time the first laws were enshrined, slavery was common and pervasive. When the Code of Hammurabi appeared about 4,100 years ago, setting out the first complete legal system, it showed a slave system in full operation. There are 282 separate laws in the code regulating most of civil life, and 35 of them concern slavery. The last in the list reads, "If a slave say to his master: 'You are not my master,' if they convict him his master shall cut off his ear." This first slave code strikes the same note over and over — a slave is not a whole person, a slave does not have the value of a "real" human being.

In the "civilized" and regulated society of ancient Babylon, if a man struck a pregnant woman so that she lost her child, the man's own daughter would be killed. If the same man struck a pregnant slave woman and she lost her child, the man had to pay her master two silver coins. A doctor botching an operation on a free man could have his hands cut off; a doctor killing a slave got off with a fine. Somehow, in our earliest civilization, when our ancestors were inventing the world that would become ours, they found that they could turn people into livestock.

Slavery thrived in ancient Mesopotamia, the "cradle of civilization." It was a major social institution in ancient Egypt, Greece, Rome and China and was generally accepted by the major religions developing at the time. Slavery is a part of both the Jewish Torah, which speaks of the Jews enslaved in Egypt and provides rules for how Jews should treat their slaves, and the Christian Bible, which admonishes slaves to submit to their masters. Slavery is also depicted in the Muslim Qur'an in the context of both Greco-Roman and Arabian cultures. Between AD 320 and AD 1453, slavery was a large part of the economy of the Byzantine Empire in the Mediterranean. Throughout history, as empires expanded, conquered people would be included in the new empires as slaves, whose work fueled the empire's further growth. As civilizations, empires and religions grew around the world, slavery flourished.

The Transatlantic Trade and American Slavery

The transatlantic slave trade fueled one of the biggest growths in global slavery. Just as the Roman and Byzantine empires had grown on the backs of newly enslaved people, this trade marked the beginning of a global Europe. Starting in the 1400s, European ships began bringing captured Africans to Europe as slaves. With the conquest and colonization of the Americas, the trade expanded to include North and South America.

The transatlantic slave trade was a triangular trade. Ships from Europe would travel to Africa loaded with manufactured goods that were traded for people captured in Africa, who were loaded onto the ships and sent to the Americas. The slaves who survived the journey across the Atlantic would be sold to the colonists, primarily for agricultural work. The ships that brought the slaves were then loaded with raw goods, like tobacco, sugar, cotton and rum, and sent back to Europe, where the process would start again. The transatlantic slave trade lasted until slavery was banned by Brazil, the last country in the Americas to do so, in 1888. An estimated 10 to 28 million people were taken from Africa during that time.[2] At the same time, a similar slave trade was taking place between Africa and North Africa, the Middle East, and the areas around the Indian Ocean. As great imperial powers emerged throughout the world, slavery grew with them and supported them.

Slavery was important to the economy of the North American colonies. While it is well known that slavery thrived in the colonies that are now the southern states of the US, slaves worked in agriculture and other jobs throughout New England and the Canadian maritime provinces as well. Enslaved Africans made up one-fifth of the population of New Amsterdam in 1664, when it was handed over to the British and renamed New York. At the time of the American Revolution in 1775, the states of Connecticut, Massachusetts, New Jersey and New York held almost 40,000 slaves.[3] However, slavery flourished mainly in the southern colonies and states. Linked to the plantation system and an explosive growth in demand for cotton, the slave population there grew to about 4 million by 1860. After slave importation was legally (if not functionally) ended in 1808, the US became the only area of the Americas to maintain and grow its slave population through natural increase rather than constant importation. The growth of the slave population in the US before 1860 meant that slave resistance and revolt was met with ever-harsher controls over slave life.

In the United States, legal ownership of slaves ended in 1865, following the Civil War and the Thirteenth Amendment to the Constitution, which abolished slavery as a legal institution. Many people believe that all slavery ended then as well, but people continued to be enslaved in the US, and in many other parts of the world. Those who think that slavery ended after the Civil War are confusing ownership with control. It became illegal for people to own slaves, but the ability to control people without owning them remained. The abolition of legal slavery did not stop them from being held in conditions of slavery; it did not stop people from being slaves.

Abolition Movements

Historically, there have been three large-scale anti-slavery movements. These movements were key to bringing about the end of different types of slavery at different points in history. The first movement, starting in 1787, was the campaign to end the slave trade and continued until the end of legal slavery in the British Empire in 1833. The second significant anti-slavery movement was in the United States, aimed at the abolition of legal slavery during the period leading up to the Civil War. The third was an international movement, at the end of the nineteenth century, to end forced labor and slavery in the Congo under King Leopold of Belgium. Today we are at the beginning of the fourth great anti-slavery movement

Slave Resistance

In spite of the violent control by slaveholders, throughout history slaves have fought back. The Roman Empire had a very large proportion of slaves in its population, mainly captives from foreign conquest and their descendants. Over a period of about seventy years, from 135 BC to 70 BC, the Roman world was rocked by three sweeping slave revolts involving many thousands of slaves. The last of these, sometimes called the Gladiator War or the War of Spartacus, began as a small uprising of enslaved gladiators that grew into an army of some 120,000. These men defeated the Roman army several times over a three-year period before being wiped out. The fear engendered by this revolt led to extremely harsh punishments.

A slave revolt in the French colony of Saint Domingue led to a revolution, freedom for the slaves there and the founding of an independent Haiti. The self-educated ex-slave Toussaint L'Ouverture shaped a slave uprising that began in 1791 into a coherent campaign that ultimately defeated both a British force and a large-scale invasion of French troops sent by Napoleon. L'Ouverture died in 1802, but after further conflict the French withdrew and the Haitian Republic was proclaimed in 1804.

The success of the Haitian revolution instilled great fear in the slaveholders of the Southern United States, and they increased their oppression and watchfulness over slaves. In spite of that watchfulness, more than 250 small-scale revolts took place in the South. The most significant of these was the one led by the slave Nat Turner in 1831 in Virginia. More than fifty slaves took part in this bloody revolt and fifty-seven white men, women and children were killed. In the aftermath of the revolt, the control of slaves became more tightly regulated.

— the movement to eradicate slavery throughout the world, once and for all.

In England in 1787, a handful of Quakers and a young Anglican, Thomas Clarkson, who had just graduated from university, formed the first human rights organization. Their goal was the complete abolition of the slave trade and the emancipation of slaves throughout the empire. Although England itself had few slaves — unlike the Caribbean colonies and the Thirteen Colonies — English capitalists and ships were deeply involved in the slave trade. In time, this little group became known as the Anti-Slavery Society. By 1791 the society started a vigorous human rights campaign with 1,300 local branches across Great Britain. The campaign boycotted products that resulted from slavery, such as sugar from colonies in the Caribbean. It also raised public awareness, circulated petitions and lobbied the government to change the laws in order to outlaw the transatlantic slave trade, which it succeeded in doing in 1807. After the end of the Napoleonic wars, the campaign began again, this time with the aim of abolishing slavery itself. Another hard-fought struggle brought about the end of legal slavery in the British Empire in 1833.

This first abolition movement spilled over into a second movement in the United States during the early part of the nineteenth century. It included the Quakers, abolitionists such as William Lloyd Garrison and the escaped slave Frederick Douglass. These abolitionists worked tirelessly to change the mind of the American public about slavery. They raised awareness of the cruelty of slavery,

The Little Book That Started the Great War

Uncle Tom's Cabin, a novel by Harriet Beecher Stowe, centers on the lives of several slaves in the American South in the early 1850s. The story follows the protagonist, Uncle Tom, as he is sold to increasingly evil masters. Stowe wrote the book with the hopes that it would convince readers in the North that slavery needed to end. She succeeded in galvanizing huge public support for the abolitionist movement. When she met President Abraham Lincoln, he reportedly said, "So you're the little woman who wrote the book that started this Great War."

Uncle Tom's Cabin sold an astounding 300,000 copies in the US and 1.5 million copies worldwide the first year it was published. The text was translated into every major language and read by people all over the world.[4] The book was also turned into a stage play that toured American cities and towns. For many US citizens at the time, their first experience of the theater was attending a performance of *Uncle Tom's Cabin*.

helped runaway slaves to freedom in the North and in Canada, and lobbied hard in opposition to laws such as the Fugitive Slave Act, which mandated that escaped slaves be returned to their masters. British abolitionists aided the American abolitionists as well. The growing popular support of the abolition movement was one of the key factors that led to the US Civil War and the end of legal slavery.

In addition to helping change the laws about slavery, the abolition movements of the late eighteenth and nineteenth centuries helped change how the public thought about slavery. Many of the key arguments supporting slavery, in both Europe and the Americas, focused on how it was essential to the economic success of the slaver nations. It is true that the combined value of slaves was enormous, representing a vast capital investment, and their work produced huge profits. The abolition movement shifted the focus, presenting slavery as a moral issue. This redefinition occurred when abolitionists were able to lead the public to recognize the humanity of slaves and to empathize with their suffering. One of the most famous images from the British abolition movement is that of a chained slave on one knee with his arms raised, asking, "Am I not a man and a brother?"

What was revolutionary about the calls of the abolitionists is that they were asking everyone to see the world from the slave's perspective, to recognize a common humanity with people who were legally defined as subhuman. Given that slavery was perfectly legal and recognized in the US Constitution, many people found these ideas extremely strange and often shocking. The power of *Uncle Tom's Cabin* was that it left little doubt in the reader's mind of the essential humanity of the slaves, especially when contrasted to the inhumanity of the slaveholders.

Slavery continued in different forms in the US and around the world after the Civil War and the emancipation of the American slaves. Following the end of the slave trade and the end of legal slavery in the US, the English Anti-Slavery Society continued functioning and took up the cause of slavery in the Congo in Central Africa.

King Leopold II of Belgium established the Congo

Free State in 1885 and ran it as a personal business. This business used slave labor to produce rubber, a product in high demand. Whole villages were enslaved to collect rubber in the forests and those who failed to collect the required amount would have a hand or a foot chopped off. Anti-slavery activists used newspapers and a new technology, photography, to expose the terrible conditions in the Congo. Photographs taken there showed evidence of torture and mutilation of slaves. Activists presented slideshows of the slaves in the Congo at more than 600 public events in Europe and the US over the course of two years. In 1908, after years of pressure from journalists and activists, the Belgian Parliament convinced King Leopold to surrender his private Congo Free State to Belgium, ending slavery there. The death toll during the period of enslavement and exploitation is estimated to be as high as 10 million people and is widely considered genocide.[5]

By the time the problem of slavery in the Congo was addressed, two key changes had taken place in how the public viewed slavery. The first change was legal. Slavery became illegal when countries outlawed first the slave trade, then the practice of slavery itself. By the early twentieth century, slavery was illegal across Europe, North America and South America, with other countries all over the world following suit. The second change was that slavery became hidden; it became a crime that was concealed. Because of the public redefinition of slavery as morally wrong and the fact that it was illegal, slavery moved into the shadows. There were no longer public auctions of slaves or public documentation of slave holdings. Slavery became a crime that took place away from public view, like rape and murder.

Slavery After Emancipation

Legal emancipation in the US didn't stop Southern planters from re-enslaving thousands of African Americans. This time, instead of slavery, it was called peonage, a form of debt bondage. African Americans were duped or coerced into signing contracts as field workers or sharecroppers. The farm owners would "hold" their pay, and they were obligated to make all their purchases from a company store, using tickets or orders rather than money. When their annual contracts expired, they found that the crops they raised almost never paid the debts they owed. Although it was often apparent that these so-called debts were imaginary or impossibly inflated, the penalty for nonpayment was jail. Local police helped to enforce this control over the lives of African Americans, just as they had done when slavery was legal. The only alternative was to stay on the land and try to work off the debt, which never seemed to lessen or disappear. Worse, the debt passed from parent to child, binding families to the land with no hope of advancement or escape. Each year became a frustrating, spirit-crushing effort to break even. Begun with the blessing of President Andrew Johnson immediately after the Civil War, peonage was practiced across the South and upheld for decades by local and federal governments. A full federal ban on peonage was not passed until 1948, and it persisted across much of the South well into the 1960s.

While both the US government and the American people generally ignored peonage, another form of slavery was very much on Americans' minds in the first decades of the twentieth century. Large numbers of foreign-born women immigrants were being exploited in many areas of the workforce, and some were being forced into prostitution. At this time prostitution was rapidly expanding in the growing industrial cities, and it was controlled by the same criminal organizations that ran corrupt local governments. Operating from the premise that white women — both immigrant and native-born — were being either lured or abducted, sold and forced into prostitution, reformers and religious groups mounted a nation-wide campaign. Using the term "white slavery" to describe this systematic sexual coercion and exploitation of young women, religious leaders and journalists waged war against pimps and procurers. The campaign captured the imagination of middle-class white America, and, inevitably, legislation for safeguarding endangered womanhood was introduced. At best, the laws were misguided; at worst they were used as an excuse for racial oppression and the wholesale deportation of recent immigrants.

Global Slavery in the Twentieth Century

After World War I, slavery continued unabated around the world, largely ignored by the international community. Different forms of debt bondage, akin to feudalism, were common throughout India, Pakistan, Nepal and

Bangladesh. In China the sale of children to be slave servants accounted for thousands of new slaves each year. Across East and West Africa, similar forms of child slavery continued. The *restavec* system of child slaves in Haiti carried on throughout the twentieth century and still enslaves 100,000 or more children today.[6] Restavec derives from the French, *rester avec*, meaning "to stay with." Poor children from the rural areas work as domestic servants in the homes of better-off urban relatives or other families. In the countries bordering the Sahara desert, Bedouin tribes like the Tuareg continued their age-old practice of capturing slaves in sub-Saharan Africa and then selling them in Arab markets in the north.

Into the early twentieth century, the slave market of Mecca was known for its size and diversity. In a sad joining of slavery and religion, people from across the Muslim world would bring a slave with them on their religious pilgrimage, or Hajj, to Mecca and sell the slave there to help finance the trip. Tribal chiefs and rulers across East Africa also supplied slaves to the market in Mecca. In West Africa slavery also joined with religion in the Trokosi temples. Sins could be atoned for if a young girl was given over to the Trokosi priests to be used as a servant and for sexual purposes. In India as well, young girls were forced to be devadasi slaves in some Hindu temples, where they would cook and clean and then be prostituted by the priests.

In South America slaves were used to mine gold and emeralds and to grow and harvest sugar. Slaves there were also used to tap rubber trees in the jungles and were tortured and mutilated when they failed to meet quotas, just as slaves had been in the Congo. The flow of rubber and sugar, and especially the arrival of cocoa grown by slaves, sparked a new concern among European and North American consumers about slavery. Until about 1915, some 97,000 slaves were shipped from the Portuguese colony of Angola to the islands of São Tomé and Principe off the west coast of Africa to work on large cocoa plantations run by Europeans. When consumers became aware of the situation, petitions and boycotts were organized. While the use of slaves in the islands stopped with the end of colonization, slaves are still used today in cocoa production in West Africa.

The twentieth century also saw a vast increase in the amount of state-sponsored slavery. Under the Nazi dictatorship in Germany, more than 10 million people were enslaved and put to work in factories and fields. The Nazi regime was extremely racist and very frank about its intention to enslave what it considered to be subhuman people.

During World War II, the Japanese military enslaved thousands of civilian non-combatant Philippine, Korean, Thai, Vietnamese and Chinese women and children as forced prostitutes for use by soldiers. Large "comfort stations" that amounted to state-run brothels were established in all the countries occupied by the Japanese military. Approximately 200,000 women were enslaved in this way. In addition to the serial rape they suffered, many were tortured and murdered. Collectively known as "comfort women," the massive scale of their degradation and abuse is staggering.

In the Soviet Union some 18 million people, arrested for their political or religious beliefs, were enslaved in prison camps that operated farms, mines, foundries and factories from 1930 until the 1960s. These prisoners were often worked to death and were sometimes used to make products, such as cars, which would be exported abroad. This practice continues in modern-day China, where the government maintains a large system of prison factories.

An Explosion of Slavery

Although there was widespread slavery before World War II, it tended to be restricted to smaller, and often diminishing, populations. The increase in the number of potential slaves and the subsequent fall in price of slaves set the stage for a great expansion in global slavery. In the countries where it already existed, slavery increased. In the countries where it had died out, there was a resurgence. This was especially true when the Cold War ended in 1989. The collapse of the iron curtain that rigidly separated so many countries and the loosening of travel restrictions meant that people and products began to flow in large numbers across borders. Criminals rapidly took advantage of this situation and a revitalized slave trade emerged. This modern slave trade is commonly referred to as human trafficking.

Finally, the late twentieth century saw slavery repeat some of its oldest historical patterns, coming full circle from ancient Babylonia to modern-day Bosnia, Sudan and Sri Lanka. Human slavery was born in conflict, and wars today still unlock slavery and set it loose on threatened populations. With armed conflict often comes a collapse of the rule of law, making many people vulnerable to enslavement. This was clearly demonstrated when citizens of the former Yugoslavia were forced into slavery as the country descended into chaos and civil war in the 1990s. In Sri Lanka, Sudan, Liberia and other parts of the world, children are also enslaved as child soldiers, due, in part, to the proliferation of small arms across the developing world.

Slavery changed in the twentieth century, evolving into its modern form that has devalued individual slaves and increased both their disposability and the profits to be made by the slaveholder. Governments, religious groups and individuals enslaved millions of people, and continue to do so. The end of the twentieth century brought the realization that slavery had grown into a global problem.

Chapter 3
Types of Slavery

The world of new slavery is both simple and complex. It is simple because the basic facts of slavery remain the same for all slaves: the loss of free will and control by violence, no payment and economic exploitation. It is complex because while slavery has always had those facts at its center, it is packaged in many different ways. There are families who have been in slavery for generations, and people who were just enslaved last week. There are governments that enslave their own citizens, and there is slavery caused when environmental destruction pushes poor people over the edge. Both slaveholders and communities that turn a blind eye to slavery have thousands of ways to conceal and justify this crime. The most common types of modern slavery fall into three main groups: human trafficking, debt bondage and forced labor.

Human Trafficking
In North America and Western Europe, slavery is almost always linked to human trafficking, the transporting of a person into slavery. Human trafficking is the term that is

used to describe how people are recruited or kidnapped and then moved across borders, or even over distances within a country, into a situation of enslavement. Laws and treaties aimed at controlling the international slave trade go back to the early nineteenth century, but in the 1990s a new understanding of the crime of human trafficking emerged. In 2000, after several years of negotiation, the United Nations put forward the Convention against Transnational Organized Crime, and its Protocol to Prevent, Suppress and Punish Trafficking in Persons, Especially Women and Children. An important point about the 2000 Trafficking Protocol is that for the first time the international community has an agreed standard definition of trafficking in persons.

Put simply, trafficking is the crime of carrying someone into slavery by force or fraud. It is a crime whether or not the person agrees to go with the trafficker. There

The Definition of Human Trafficking

The Trafficking Protocol defines trafficking in persons as the action of recruitment, transportation, transfer, harboring, or receipt of persons:

- by means of the threat or use of force, coercion, abduction, fraud, deception, abuse of power or vulnerability, or giving payments or benefits to a person in control of the victim
- for the purposes of exploitation, which includes exploiting the prostitution of others, sexual exploitation, forced labor, slavery or similar practices, and the removal of organs.

The protocol makes clear that consent of the victim is irrelevant where illicit means have been used.[1]

are three underlying factors at work that foster trafficking. The first factor is that within the origin countries (where trafficked people are recruited) there is a seemingly endless supply of victims available for exploitation. Second, within the destination countries (where trafficked people are sent) there is an endless demand for the victims' services. The third factor is that organized criminal networks, some large and some small, have taken control of this "supply and demand" situation to traffic and enslave people in order to generate enormous profits for themselves.

Smuggling and Trafficking

Many victims of trafficking begin their journey by consenting to be smuggled from one country to another. Because of this, the difference between smuggling and trafficking in persons has been an area of some confusion. Smuggling and trafficking both involve moving human beings for profit, but in smuggling the relationship between migrants and smugglers usually ends on arrival in the destination country. The criminal's profit is derived from the process of smuggling the migrant alone. In cases of trafficking, the smuggling is just a prelude and conduit into enslavement. The United Nations Convention against Transnational Organized Crime holds that smuggling of migrants is the:

- procurement of illegal entry
- into a State of which the person is not a national or a permanent resident

- to obtain direct or indirect financial or other material benefit.[2]

By this definition, many of the activities of human traffickers (such as using fraudulent travel documents) are also smuggling, but trafficking goes beyond simply the "procurement of illegal entry into a State." Put another way, human trafficking is smuggling *plus* coercion or deception at the beginning of the process and enslavement at the end. This means that law enforcement officers who encounter cases in progress may not know whether smuggling or trafficking is occurring.

Because many trafficking victims believe that they are only being smuggled, they often pay to be enslaved. That's why, ironically, most slaves in North America and Europe are "volunteers." Today the slave-takers rarely have to coerce or kidnap their victims. All the criminals have to do is open a door to "opportunity" and the slaves walk in. Slave recruiters all over the world appear friendly and full of news about good jobs with good pay. There may even be a little money for the rest of the family as an "advance" on the big wages to be earned. This helps ease the victims out of their homes and into the pipeline that will deliver them into slavery.

Once they are in the pipeline, their documents are taken away "for safekeeping." The transit house, where they stay at night, is locked up "to keep everyone safe." They are fed little, and the "boss" keeps them awake most of the night. Within a few days, sleep deprivation, hunger and isolation take their toll, and confusion and dependence set in. Disoriented, they are constantly reminded that soon they'll be working at regular jobs in the rich destination country. Thinking they are being smuggled, they have no idea that at this point they are, in fact, slaves; and they walk, ride, fly or float further into bondage. Once they arrive in the new country, far from family, without any proof of identity, unable to speak the language, hungry, confused and now threatened, they discover that they are, in fact, slaves.

Trafficking Victims

Because the crimes of slavery and human trafficking are hidden crimes, there is no precise count of the number of victims. It is estimated that as many as 800,000 people are trafficked between countries and millions more within individual countries each year.[3] Approximately 17,000 people are trafficked annually into the United States, and between 2,000 and 3,000 into Canada. These numbers are thought to have decreased since the tightening of borders and security after the terrorist attacks of September 11, 2001. Across the globe, the International Labor Organization estimates that there are 2.4 million people who have been trafficked into slavery. The ILO breaks down the total number and estimates the numbers of victims that are trafficked into and enslaved in each region of the world, as well as the profits gained from those victims (see page 46).

The large number of trafficked people is not surprising given a basic rule of human trafficking: trafficked people flow from poorer countries to richer countries. In

Region	Number of Victims Trafficked into Region	Profit ($ billions)
Asia and the Pacific	1,360,000	9.7
Industrialized Countries (Europe, USA, Canada)	270,000	15.5
Latin America and the Caribbean	250,000	1.3
Middle East and North Africa	230,000	1.5
Transition Countries (Eastern Europe)	200,000	3.4
Sub-Saharan Africa	130,000	0.159

Trafficking Victims and Trafficking Profits by Region, 2005

Source: "Forced Labor Statistics," *A Global Alliance against Forced Labor*, ILO, Geneva, 2005.

the very poorest countries of the world, such as Chad and Mali in Africa, young people are trafficked into domestic service or agriculture in nearby richer countries such as Ivory Coast or Ghana. At the same time, young people from Ivory Coast, Ghana or Nigeria are tricked and trafficked to even richer countries in Africa, or sent to Europe and North America. Young women from Eastern

European countries are tricked by the promise of jobs in North America or Japan and then forced into prostitution on arrival. The poor of the Philippines and South America are trafficked to Japan or to North America. In large countries, such as China or India, children and adults are trafficked from poorer regions to richer regions of the same country, joining trafficking victims from Nepal or Burma.

The numbers of people trafficked are shocking. What is even more astonishing is that this is a crime that normally goes unpunished. In the United States, for example, about 17,000 people are trafficked into the country and enslaved each year. There are also about 17,000 murders in the United States each year, one of the highest rates in the world. Murder is the ultimate crime against human dignity, but slavery comes a close second, especially considering the other crimes associated with it, such as rape and torture. The national success rate in the US for solving murder cases is about 70 percent; approximately 12,000 murders are "cleared" each year, meaning they are prosecuted or resolved in some way. Compare that to the "clear-up" rate for human trafficking. According to the US government's own numbers, the annual percentage of trafficking and slavery cases solved is less than 1 percent. In 2005, the Department of Justice brought charges against 118 people for human trafficking and slavery; only 45 were convicted. In fact, about one-third of the handful of slaves freed in the United States each year come to liberty because a neighbor sees something he or she just can't ignore.

A Mexican Girl's Journey into Slavery in the US

Sandra Bearden, a twenty-seven-year-old married homemaker in a comfortable suburb of Laredo, Texas, wanted someone to do the housework and help look after her young son, but she didn't want to pay much. So she drove across the border to a small, poor village near Vera Cruz, Mexico, where she was introduced to Maria and her parents. Maria was only twelve; she had not had much schooling and dreamed of getting an education — a dream that her parents encouraged but could do nothing to help her achieve. Sandra offered Maria a job, as well as the chance to attend school. Maria's parents gave their permission and Sandra smuggled Maria across the border.

Once in Laredo, Maria was dragged into hell. Sandra Bearden used violence and terror to squeeze work and obedience from the child. From early morning till mid-afternoon, Maria cooked, cleaned, scrubbed and polished. If she dozed off from exhaustion, or if Sandra decided she wasn't working fast enough, Sandra would blast pepper spray into Maria's eyes. Sandra broke a broom over Maria's back and a few days later, a bottle against her head.

When Maria wasn't working, Sandra would chain her to a pole in the backyard without food or water. A 2.5 meter-high (eight feet) concrete fence kept her hidden from neighbors. After chaining her, Sandra would sometimes force Maria to eat dog feces. Then Maria would be left alone till the next morning, when the work and torture would begin again. Maria would fade in

Debt Bondage

Debt bondage has much in common with the slavery of the past. It works like this: when a crisis occurs, like a serious illness or a crop failure, poor families do not have the resources to buy medicine or enough food. In this desperate situation, the slaveholder steps in and offers to loan the money or food needed to keep the family alive. Very often family members know that they are risking and out of consciousness from dehydration and in her hunger sometimes scoop dirt into her mouth. Like most slaves in America, Maria was in shock, disoriented, isolated and completely dependent.

One of the Beardens' neighbors had to do some work on his roof, which probably saved Maria's life. Looking down over the high concrete wall, he saw a small girl who was chained up and whimpering, so he called the police.

The police found Maria chained hand and foot, covered in cuts and bruises, suffering from dehydration and exposure. Police photos show one of her eyes bloodied and infected, and thick welts and scars on her skin. She had not eaten in four days. When Sandra Bearden was charged with enslaving Maria, the district attorney said, "This is the worst case I've ever seen, worse than any murder." Policeman Jay Reece explained that he tried to remove the chains from Maria's arms with bolt cutters but couldn't. As he tried to move her arms to cut the chains, she couldn't bear his touch because she was in so much pain. "I've never seen anything like it before," Reece said, and sitting in the witness box, he began to cry.

Unlike most slaveholders in America, Bearden was caught and convicted of multiple offenses, including human trafficking and slavery. She is serving a life sentence. Like most slaves, Maria got nothing, except the fare for the twelve-hour bus ride home. She had just turned thirteen.

slavery, but take the offer in order to save the family from starvation or death from disease.

The enslavement comes through the terms of the loan. These families own nothing of value, so the slaveholder requires them to put up their own lives as collateral against the debt. The slaveholder loans them enough money to buy the food or medicine they need, but then gets all their work, the complete productive capacity of the family, as collateral. None of the family's work repays the loan; it belongs to the slaveholder as long as the family owes the debt. Since the family normally can't earn any money except through the work it does, and since the slaveholder already owns that work as his collateral, the debt can never be repaid. What's more, the debt passes from husband to wife and from parent to child. This may be one of the oldest types of slavery in the world, dating back thousands of years. Under debt bondage the slaveholder provides food to the family and sometimes a place to live as well, but the food is usually just enough to keep from starving and the shelter is minimal. In Nepal, India, Bangladesh and Pakistan more than 10 million people are held in this type of slavery.

In the Northern Indian state of Uttar Pradesh, entire villages are enslaved through debt bondage, where every man, woman and child is forced to work in the fields or in rock quarries. The children are not allowed to go to school and the slaveholders sexually assault the women. Cut off from the world, born into a reality in which their whole community is enslaved, bonded families may have no idea that freedom is possible. Debt bondage and slavery are illegal in India, but rich and powerful farmers and moneylenders bribe poorly paid police to look the other way. Debt bondage has also been practiced for so long that it is regarded as normal. Slaveholders justify debt bondage by saying that the families aren't capable of taking care of themselves and insist that this isn't really slavery, since they are just waiting for the family to repay their debt.

Forced Labor

While all slavery is a kind of forced labor, this term has the special meaning of slavery that is practiced not by a person but by a government or some other official group. Historically, many countries, especially the European empires of the nineteenth century, enslaved millions of people in their African and Asian colonies. The worst violator was probably King Leopold of Belgium, whose brutal slavery in the Congo touched off the third major anti-slavery movement.

Since the horrific events in the Congo at the end of the nineteenth century, other countries have forced their citizens into slavery. Today the country of Uzbekistan in Central Asia sends most of its school and college students into the cotton fields for up to three months each year. Cotton is the country's main export and worth over $1 billion. The youths have no choice about doing this work and are paid little or nothing for their labor. In China much of the national penal system has been converted into factories for the export trade. Given that there is no legal process that protects rights, and that people can be arrested for exercising free speech or practicing their religion, large numbers of the workers caught up in the state-owned prison factories can only be described as slaves. A large proportion of the goods made in these factories are exported to North America.

In Burma in 1990 the National League for Democracy, led by Aung San Suu Kyi, won a landslide victory in free elections. Refusing to give up power, the military dictatorship arrested her and declared martial law. Since then, the country (renamed Myanmar) has been operated as a private business benefiting the generals who run the government. As schools and hospitals crumble, the generals and other officers become rich by forcing whole villages to work for them. Mining and lumber cutting is carried out at gunpoint and with no pay. Instead of trucks, thousands of people are used as pack animals for the army. Soldiers take whatever they want, often attacking and raping women. A soldier interviewed by a human rights organization in 2003 described what he saw as his unit moved into a village:

> I heard a lot of noise from one house. There were some women screaming and crying. Two women came out of the house. Two soldiers started raping them. I knew the soldiers; they were [names deleted]. I saw this with my own eyes from about twenty yards away. There were three other women in the house with five more soldiers, and there was a lot of shouting and crying inside the house. After the two soldiers outside let the two women go, five soldiers and three women came out of the house and all the women ran past me into the jungle. The men were laughing and saying, "Oh how nice," after the women. They also stole some necklaces from the house. We stayed in that village for two weeks. We killed all the pigs in the village and dried the meat. As we left, we burned down the whole village.[4]

The United Nations has condemned Burma and the United States and other countries have enforced sanctions against the country.

Chapter 4
Slavery Around the World

The 27 million slaves in the world today live in many different situations and different types of slavery. Here is a snapshot of slavery in six different countries: Japan, Brazil, Mauritania, the United Arab Emirates (UAE), India and the United States.

Japan

Japan, an advanced, wealthy economic powerhouse, has an enormous problem with slavery and human trafficking. Slavery in Japan is fueled by racism, sexism and government complacency. The Japanese population is one of the most law-abiding in the world, with a robbery rate of 1.3 per 100,000 people compared with a rate in the US that is nearly 180 times greater. Yet in Japan, where the police patrol every block of the cities and the citizens are among the world's safest, slavery, especially sexual slavery, flourishes.

The sex industry in Japan is vast, generating billions of dollars a year. Referred to euphemistically as the "entertainment industry," it includes brothels, strip clubs, bathhouses and street prostitution. (Prostitution is illegal. However, it is narrowly defined as intravaginal intercourse in exchange for money, which leaves the door open for the sale of many other sexual services.) The government has a special "entertainer visa" that is used to bring in foreign women to work in the sex industry. In 2003, approximately 80,000 "entertainers" came from the Philippines and 40,000 came from other countries, including the US, China and Russia. Over the years, around 40,000 women have come from Latin America on entertainer visas. But these visas are just one part of the trafficking problem. Thousands more foreign women trapped in slavery in Japan are there on over-stayed visas and tourist visas. There is also a high rate of marriage between Japanese men and foreign women. While some of these marriages are legitimate, many are fake marriages set up by traffickers. Taking into account these numbers and recruitment methods, a conservative estimate of the total number of foreign women enslaved in sexual slavery in Japan is 25,000.

The US State Department releases an annual Trafficking in Persons Report, which ranks countries in the following way: tier 1 countries are those doing a good job dealing with human trafficking; tier 2 countries are those that are trying to deal with the problem but are not doing enough; and tier 3 countries are those with serious human trafficking problems that are doing nothing. In the 2004 report, Japan appeared on the tier 2 Watch List, along with poor, war-torn countries like Serbia, Tajikistan, and Ivory Coast, meaning it was in danger of being classified as tier 3, where sanctions can apply.

The Japanese government scrambled to enact laws and increase policing of the entertainment industry, but their actions were largely ineffective. Out of the estimated 25,000 slaves in Japan, the number of victims found and protected rose from six to twenty-five — one-tenth of 1 percent of the victims.

How can a crime that often involves the serial rape,

Journey from Thailand

Noi came from a poor community in rural Thailand. At age fifteen, seeking to escape rape and sexual abuse in her foster family, she found a foreign labor agent in Bangkok who advertised well-paid waitress jobs in Japan. She flew to Japan, later learning that she had entered the country on a tourist visa under a false identity. On her arrival, she was taken to a karaoke bar, a front for the brothel, where the owner raped her, subjected her to a blood test and then bought her. "I felt like a piece of flesh being inspected," she recounted.

The brothel madam told Noi that she had to pay off a debt of over ten thousand US dollars for her travel expenses. She was warned that girls who tried to escape were brought back by the Japanese mafia, severely beaten and had their debts doubled. The only way to pay off the debt was to see as many clients as quickly as possible. Some clients beat the girls with sticks, belts and chains. If the victims returned crying, they were beaten by the madam and told that they must have provoked the client.

The prostitutes routinely used drugs before sex, "so that we didn't feel so much pain." Most clients refused to wear condoms. The victims were given birth control pills to avoid pregnancy and any pregnancies that did occur were terminated with home abortions. Victims who managed to pay off their debts and work independently were often arrested by the police, fined, imprisoned and then raped by the police before being deported. Noi finally managed to escape with the help of a Japanese NGO.[1]

assault and kidnapping of thousands of women continue to be ignored? In part, the answer is that in Japan there are no laws prohibiting racial or gender discrimination. Domestic violence only became illegal in 2002 and police routinely ignore complaints of assaults on women by their husbands. In addition, researchers contend that the Japanese police are tolerant of organized crime, which often includes human trafficking.[2] This tolerance helps to explain the low levels of detection of human trafficking, even when there are five police stations with officers operating around the clock for every square mile area in urban Japan.

The Japanese government does not ignore all exploitation of women, however. Over the last decade, some Japanese schoolgirls practiced *enjo kosai* or "compensated dating." Using their mobile phones, girls between the ages of 15 and 17 would arrange dates with older Japanese men. The dates could simply be for coffee or could include sexual contact, and the girls were paid for their time. When the practice came to light, there was a public outcry about the exploitation of these girls by Japanese men. Legislation was immediately enacted and protections were put in place. At the same time this controversy raged, thousands of foreign women, many the same age as the Japanese schoolgirls, were trapped in an endless cycle of sexual exploitation and violence in forced prostitution. Japan's complacency in regard to the sex industry has made it one of the top destinations in the world for sex trafficking of foreign women, according to the US State Department.[3]

Brazil

Brazil is a country with few of the advantages of Japan when it comes to policing slavery. It is a vast country — the fifth largest in the world both in area and in population — that contains much of the Amazon basin and a wild frontier in the west. All along that frontier, slaves are used to cut down the trees of the great Amazon rain forest, to hack away at sugar cane, to clear brush for cattle farms, to burn timber to produce charcoal and to do any other dirty and dangerous work.

In the lush forests of western Brazil are wretched camps where slaves chop wood, stack it in hive-shaped ovens the height of a tall man, and slowly burn it into charcoal. Co-author Kevin Bales described it in this way in 1999:

> All around the camp for a mile or so the land has been stripped and gouged. The exposed earth is red and eroded. The tree stumps, the great patches of burned-over grass and wood, the trenches and holes, and the ever-present pall of smoke turn it into a battleground. The wreckage of the forest is everywhere. Covered with black soot and gray ash and shiny with sweat, the workers move like ghosts in and out of the smoke around the ovens. All the workers I saw were just muscle, bone and scars, every bit of fat had been burned off by the heat and effort. The overpowering, choking smoke colors and flavors everything. The eucalyptus smoke, full of the sharp oils the tree makes, is acrid and burns

the eyes, nose and throat. All of the charcoal workers cough constantly, hacking and spitting and trying to clear lungs that are always full of smoke, ash, heat and charcoal dust. If they live long enough they will suffer from black-lung disease. [...] The workers hover on the edge of heat stroke and dehydration. Sometimes, when we spoke to them, they were confused as if their brains had been baked. The workers who empty the ovens stay almost naked, but this exposes their skin to burns. Sometimes standing on the piles of charcoal they will stumble and the charcoal will give way and they will fall into red-hot coals. All of the charcoal workers I met had hands, arms and legs crisscrossed with ugly burn scars, some still swollen and festering.[4]

The charcoal burners are just one kind of slave in Brazil, and the problem is well known. Until 2002, however, the government did very little except to practice a vigorous system of denials and obfuscation. The influence of rich landowners was too strong, and the slaves themselves were seen as irrelevant and disposable. In agriculture, land clearances, mining, charcoal production and prostitution, men, women and children lost their free will and sometimes their lives to the slaveholders.

Brazil also has a terrible and tragic history of slavery. From the beginning of colonization until late in the nineteenth century, slaves were transported from Africa to Brazil in huge numbers. As many as ten times more

Africans were shipped to Brazil than to the United States — approximately 10 million people — but because the death rate on the sugar plantations was so high, the slave population of Brazil was never more than half that of the US. It also took much longer to bring legal slavery to an end in Brazil. It was the last country in the Americas to abolish legal slavery, with full emancipation in May 1888.

Official government reports admit that there are 25,000 slaves in Brazil (the same as the estimate for Japan), but the top anti-slavery official in the capital concedes the number today is probably closer to 50,000.

Dramatic changes began to occur in Brazil after the election of Luiz Inacio Lula da Silva as president in October 2002. Known everywhere as "Lula," he had a background in organized labor that predisposed him to take action against slavery. He also understood poverty. Lula grew up in a very poor family, left school after the fourth grade, went to work in a copper smelter at age fourteen, lost a finger in an auto factory accident at nineteen, and then worked his way up in trade union politics. Within four months of taking office, Lula set up the National Commission for the Eradication of Slave Labor as a permanent part of the government and announced the National Plan for the Eradication of Slavery. The commission brought together all relevant government agencies, the police and national law enforcement and the anti-slavery and human rights organizations that had been carrying most of the weight up to that time.

The National Plan tightened the laws against slavery and increased the penalties for slaveholding. A radical proposal to expropriate the land belonging to slave-holders, without compensation, was put forward. Expropriated land would then be distributed to poor farmers who desperately need land. Providing access to land and a better chance at employment would prevent workers from falling back into conditions of slavery. Along the same logic, there would also be a "dirty list" of any people or companies that used slave labor that would exclude them from receiving any sort of government funds, grants or credits. Since much of the process of opening and developing land relies on government tax credits or support, this would drive slave-using companies and individuals out of that business. Most important in the short run was improving the Special Mobile Inspection Groups — the anti-slavery squads. These teams were increased in number, given good four-wheel-drive trucks and, very importantly, linked to new "mobile courts." These mobile courts could impose immediate fines, freeze bank accounts and seize assets. This meant it was much easier to force farm owners to pay freed slaves the money they were owed within hours of their rescue.

There were immediate and dramatic results from the National Plan. In 2003 the number of slaves freed more than doubled to 4,879, and there was hope that the government might actually hit its target of eradicating slavery by 2006. Sadly, the number of newly liberated slaves fell in 2004 to 2,745. The fall in numbers was due, in part, to slaveholders realizing that they could no longer operate without risk of arrest and that they needed to hide their slaves. Slaveholders also began to respond with violence to the government's campaign. In late 2003 there was a rise in the use of violence and intimidation against those working to stop slave labor, especially in rural areas. Anti-slavery activists in one state had to leave the area after receiving repeated death threats. In January 2004 three officials from the labor ministry and their driver were murdered while carrying out investigations of farms.

If there is one thing that is disappointing about the Brazilian government's campaign against slavery, it is the lack of convictions and the low fines given out to those who are caught. True, the number of freed slaves shot up in 2005 to 4,133, the "dirty list" began to see government money denied to violators, and companies on the list began to look to anti-slavery groups, like the UN's International Labor Organization (ILO), for advice about cleaning up their supply chains. But even these positive achievements leave critical steps untaken. Although more than 600 rural landlords have been caught with slaves, none of them are in prison, none have had property confiscated, and many continue the practice. The Brazilian legislature is still debating whether it is constitutional to confiscate the property of slaveholders. More than $3 million was paid to freed slaves in 2005, but reported cases can take up to forty days to be investigated and many freed slaves are being re-enslaved. There are now seven active mobile squads, but it is impossible for them to cover 8.5 million square kilometers (3.3 million square miles) of territory.

Brazil is on the right course, and compared with virtually every other country in the world, it is advanced in the fight against slavery. What is needed now is a final push. A government that can free 4,000 to 5,000 slaves a year can eradicate slavery within its borders if it devotes the will and resources to the job.

Mauritania

The slavery found in Mauritania today resembles the slavery found in the US in the early nineteenth century. The population of Mauritania is divided into three main groups: the ruling Berbers (or Moors), slaves and the descendents of slaves called the Haratine, and several tribal groups of black Africans, normally called Afro-Mauritanians. The Moors have practiced a type of chattel slavery — where a slave is completely owned by another person — for hundreds of years, continuing to the present day. At the same time, some Afro-Mauritanians have also kept slaves. The institution of slavery is deeply ingrained in the social structure and culture of the country.

Boubakar Ould Messaoud, a former slave and founder of an anti-slavery NGO in Mauritania, explained the situation in this way: "A captured slave knows freedom, so to keep him you have to chain him. But a Mauritanian slave, whose parents and grandparents before him were slaves, doesn't need chains. He has been brought up as a domesticated animal."[5] Today the exploitation of slavery remains; women are frequently raped by their masters, and the slaves do unpaid menial labor. If they try to flee, they are faced with violence.

Salma's Story

Salma-mint Saloum was a slave in Mauritania for more than thirty years. This is her story in her own words:

My name is Salma. I was born a slave in Mauritania in 1956. My parents were slaves, and their parents were slaves of the same family. As soon as I was old enough to walk, I was forced to work all day, every day. Even if we were sick, we had to work.

When I was still a child, I started taking care of the first wife of the head of the family and her children. Later, even if one of my own children was hurt or in danger, I didn't dare help my child, because I had to care for the master's wife's children first. I was beaten very often, with a wooden stick or leather belt. One day they were beating my mother, and I couldn't stand it. I tried to stop them. The head of the family got very angry with me. He tied my hands, and branded me with a burning iron, and hit me across the face. His ring cut my face and left a scar.

I was never allowed to go to school or learn anything more than some Qur'an verses and prayers. But I was lucky, because the eldest son of the master had gone to school away from our village and had different ideas than his father. This eldest son secretly taught me to speak French and to read and write a little. I think that everyone thought he was raping me, but he was teaching me.

Other slaves were afraid of liberty. They were afraid they wouldn't know where to go or what to do. But I always believed that I had to be free, and I think that helped me to escape. I tried to escape about ten years ago [1993]. I didn't know how close I was to Senegal, so I walked for two days in the wrong direction. I was found and sent back, and punished. My wrists and ankles were bound, then I was tied to a date tree in the middle of the family compound, and left for a week. The head of the family cut my wrists with a razor, so that I bled terribly. I still have scars on my arms.

Finally I met a man in the market who told me that Senegal was just across the river. I decided I had to try again. I ran to the river, where a man with a small wooden boat agreed to take me to Senegal. There I made my way to a safe house run by a former slave from Mauritania. I stayed in Senegal for a few years, earning my keep by doing housework. But I never felt safe. Always I was afraid that the master of the family would pay people to find me and bring me back to his house.

When I got to the US [in 1999, after smuggling herself across the Atlantic in a cargo ship], I worked braiding hair. The first time I was paid for work I had done, I cried. I had never seen a person paid for her work before in my life. It was a very good surprise.

One of the hardest things was leaving my children behind, but I knew I had to escape first. In the three years I have been here, I have been working to free my children. I paid people to find them and take them to Senegal, and now I am paying for my children to go to school. Every morning I get up early, and buy a phone card, and speak with them. They tell me they would rather die in the street than return to Mauritania. My oldest daughter is now in the United States with me. I want very much that my other children will join us. In Mauritania, I never had the right to make decisions concerning my own children. Here, it is so different.

In Mauritania, I didn't dare go to the government, because they wouldn't listen. It doesn't matter what the laws say, because they don't apply the laws. Maybe it's written that there is no slavery, but it's not true. Even in front of the president of Mauritania I can say in full voice that there is slavery in Mauritania, because now I am as free as he is.

When I first came to the US, I was afraid that I would be sent back. But then I met my lawyer, and a doctor who helped me, and Kevin Bales of Free the Slaves, and the Bellevue Program for Survivors of Torture. The judge at my asylum hearing was honest and did his job. He demanded proof, but then he listened, and paid attention. I would like to be a citizen of the United States one day, and I want my children to be citizens. Here I have freedom of expression. In Mauritania, there was no freedom of expression. In Senegal, I was afraid to speak out, because we were so close to Mauritania. Then I had to be cautious. I had to be far, far, far away. Here, now, I can speak out.[6]

In the past the government of Mauritania has abolished slavery on four occasions, most recently in 1980. Previous governments officially maintained that slavery did not exist in the country and actively suppressed any attempt to expose it, prohibiting the media from using the word *slave*. Anti-slavery activists, including Messaoud, have been jailed for their activities. Despite the fact that all slaves were allegedly freed again in 1980, most slaves never heard the news and remained in the same situation of slavery that they were born into. This situation of denial changed radically after the first free and fair elections took place in 2007. Messaoud Ould Boulkheir, an anti-slavery activist, was elected to a high position. The new democratic government included ex-slaves and members of anti-slavery groups and set out new policies aimed at eradicating slavery. One of the most important new laws made holding a slave a criminal offence. By the end of 2007 the government of Mauritania had delivered a plan for ending slavery to the international community and begun to implement it.

The United Arab Emirates

Thirty-five years ago, the United Arab Emirates, situated on the Arabian peninsula, was a poor desert country where people supported themselves by herding camels, fishing, and diving for pearls. Following the country's independence from the United Kingdom in 1971, oil production became a lucrative business and the UAE transformed itself into a modern state, the richest in the Arab world.

Growing Up as a Sex Slave

Nayla was a nine-year-old girl in Azerbaijan when her mother sold her to traffickers after her father's death. The traffickers took Nayla to Dubai, where she was forced to work as a prostitute in clubs. She worked as a sex slave for four years, until she was thirteen, when the Dubai police discovered that she was in the country illegally. Despite being an underage prostitute who had obviously been a trafficking victim, she was deported back to Azerbaijan. Once back in her home country, she did not receive any victims' assistance — instead she was prostituted for another three years, until she became pregnant. Nayla was infected with HIV while working either in Dubai or in Baku. She gave birth to an HIV-positive baby in 2005.[7]

The country is made up of seven separate emirates, each ruled by a hereditary emir, or prince. There is free health care and higher education for UAE citizens, and while Muslim women there usually wear a veil, there is little pressure to do so. The government promotes moderate Islam and there are both secular courts and Sharia courts, which hear family and religious disputes.

Probably the most famous emirate is Dubai. It is widely known as the Las Vegas or Bangkok of the Middle East, a place where the Arab world goes to party. The country's oil production, combined with the booming construction business, has led to an influx of foreign workers. Less than 20 percent of the country's 2.6 million residents are UAE citizens. The rest have come to live and work there, and up to half are from South Asia.

With the influx of workers from other countries has come abuse and exploitation. Men from India, Bangladesh and Pakistan expect to work in construction, but many find themselves in situations of slavery when they arrive. Their wages are denied for months at a time, their passports confiscated and they are compelled to pay off recruitment and travel expenses that are often inflated and can amount to more than two years' pay. Women come to the UAE from India, Sri Lanka, Bangladesh, Indonesia, Ethiopia and the Philippines for domestic work, and, similarly, many find themselves locked up with their wages withheld.[8]

In the UAE, especially in Dubai, there are also high levels of sex trafficking. The US government estimates that approximately 10,000 women are victims of sex trafficking in the UAE, coming from sub-Saharan Africa, Eastern Europe, South and East Asia, Iraq, Iran and Morocco.[9]

Not all forms of slavery in the UAE are tied to its rapid modernization; slavery has been prevalent in camel racing, a traditional sport in many Arab countries, including the UAE. Until recently, thousands of young boys, most under the age of ten, were trafficked into the country each year from places such as Pakistan, Bangladesh, Sudan and Mauritania, and were forced to work as camel jockeys. Young boys were used as jockeys because they were light. They were also more likely to scream and cry out during the race, making the camels run faster. The children were strapped to the animals and forced to ride for hours. They frequently fell off the camels and were trampled or dragged, often to death. The young jockeys were nearly starved, to keep their weight down, and were beaten often. The practice was illegal for years, but it remained widespread. In 2005 the country's rulers banned the practice once more and stepped up enforcement of the ban. The government admitted there were at least 3,000 children held in slavery in the camel-racing business and that year the government identified and repatriated 1,000 children to their home countries. Working with UNICEF, the UAE set up shelters for victims and funded services to help the children reintegrate in their home countries, but this kind of support has not always been carried out.

From a War Zone to Forced Prostitution

In late 2005 Mariam, a fifteen-year-old Iraqi girl, was tricked into going to the UAE. Her mother was killed in 2003 during the US invasion of Iraq and her father wanted her to go abroad to escape the growing violence in Iraq. Traffickers, posing as employment recruiters, promised Mariam a one-year contract as a domestic worker for a family in Dubai and paid her father $6,000 as an advance on her wages.

Instead, Mariam was forced into prostitution when she arrived in Dubai. The traffickers kept her in a house with twenty other young girls who were also forced sex workers. "I was a virgin and I didn't understand what sex was. I was told that they [the traffickers] were going to get good money for my first night with an old local man who paid for my virginity. He was aggressive and hit me all the time," Mariam explained. She experienced daily threats from the traffickers, who warned her not to try to leave. One day she managed to escape, eventually making her way back to Baghdad after spending months in forced prostitution.[10]

It is unclear how many children are still in slavery in the camel-racing industry. The children remaining in slavery in the UAE are thought by NGOs[11] to be used in illegal night-time camel races, or to have been trafficked out of the country. One change, however, is abundantly clear. Children are no longer used in officially sanctioned camel races. They have been replaced with child-sized robots, strapped to the camels' backs and operated by remote control.

While the UAE government has addressed the problem of child camel jockeys, it has failed to address the problems of sex trafficking and slavery in domestic service and construction. As a result, many victims remain in slavery, or are instead deported as criminals for being in the country illegally. This is because the law does not consider victims to be trafficked if they are over eighteen and entered the country voluntarily. As with most human trafficking, the vast majority of UAE trafficking victims enter the country voluntarily, paying traffickers to facilitate their entry, only to find themselves trapped in slavery when they arrive. This problem, however, seems to be remedied in new anti-trafficking laws passed by the rulers in late 2006.

These new laws are a good first step in abolishing slavery in the UAE, but they need to be thoroughly enforced. Prosecutions against traffickers are rare, considering the number of victims. When the 1,000 children were freed from camel racing in 2005, there were only 20 convictions. In the same year, of the estimated 10,000 women trapped in forced prostitution, only around 100 cases were reported and only 22 convictions upheld.[12] The gov-

Sexual Slavery in New Delhi

Reena was brought to India from Nepal by her maternal aunt when she was twelve years old. Shortly after she arrived, her aunt forced her into a New Delhi brothel. Reena was trapped — she knew no one who could help her and she did not speak the local language, Hindi. The brothel owner repeatedly forced her to have sex with clients, all day, every day. She often saw police officers collect money from the brothel owners whenever a new girl was brought in. The brothel owner made Reena and all the girls tell anyone who asked that they were twenty-five years old and had joined the brothel voluntarily. After spending two years trapped in the brothel, being repeatedly raped, Reena finally escaped. She now works to help other trafficking victims in India come to freedom.[13]

ernment has both the ability and the resources to end slavery and trafficking in the United Arab Emirates. Time will tell if the country's new anti-trafficking laws will help all the victims of trafficking in the country.

India

India is the world's largest democracy, but within its borders at least 10 million people are trapped in slavery. Men, women and children from the country's lowest castes are kept in domestic service, forced marriages, forced prostitution and debt bondage. Most of the 10 million slaves in India are held in debt bondage and work in brick kilns, rice mills, agriculture, quarries, fireworks production and garment factories.

Slavery persists in India because of a number of factors. These include extreme poverty, caste and ethnic discrimination, police corruption, porous borders that allow traffickers to slip through, a lack of public awareness, low arrest and prosecution rates for traffickers and slaveholders, and a high level of internal trafficking.

Police corruption is one of the biggest obstacles to reducing slavery in India. With debt bondage, corrupt police officers provide protection for the slaveholders and take bribes to thwart prosecutions. With sex trafficking, corrupt officers help transport trafficking victims and protect traffickers and their brothels.

Governments at all levels in India have consistently failed to arrest and punish traffickers and slaveholders in every type of slavery in the country. In 2005 rescuers freed 694 children in Delhi from slavery in garment factories and workshops.[14] However, there is no evidence that any arrests were made in connection with the rescues, and the criminals who enslaved these children have gone free.

One of the most obvious examples of government complacency — and even support of slavery — is the debt bondage that exists in Northern India. There, entire villages and families are trapped in a system that is often protected by police. There are few prosecutions for debt bondage, and the few cases that have been prosecuted resulted in small fines for the slaveholders.[15] On the other hand, India has an excellent law against debt bondage slavery. Unlike many countries, India has recognized the need for immediate support for freed slaves. Echoing the

Sankalp and Freedom Village

The revolution came silently to Sonebarsa. For four generations the people of this small village in Northern India had been slaves. Every day, every man, woman and child of the village worked in the stone quarries. Every day they broke rocks with hammers, the sharp stone chips flying and piercing their skin and eyes. Their world ended at the edge of the village. The slaveholder controlled their every movement. Violence rained down on the slaves when he thought someone hadn't followed orders, or for no reason at all. After four generations in slavery, there was no memory of freedom among these people, no sense that life could be any different. One day, into this hell slipped a worker from Sankalp, an anti-slavery organization.

Freedom without preparation can be a disaster. If slaves have no concept of life outside bondage, their liberation can fail. The Sankalp worker understood this and in 2001 began a long and gentle conversation with the people of Sonebarsa. Slowly, during many meetings, he described life in freedom, telling stories of how people in other villages had joined together to break free of the slaveholders. It took months for the flame of hope to flicker to life in the village, but finally the enslaved workers were ready.

Work stopped, and the slaveholder and his thugs came to drive the villagers back to work in the quarry. This time, instead of frightened slaves, they found the villagers united and backed up by workers from Sankalp. When the thugs tried to beat the slaves, they were pelted with stones. Shocked, the slaveholders retreated, but in the dead of the night they returned and burned the village to the ground. A baby died when his home collapsed in flames. The villagers lost all their food, their clothes and their meager possessions. They lost everything except their freedom.

The villagers trudged to a nearby plot of land and began to build. As quarry workers they knew how to shape stone and build huts, and a new village was born. Sankalp workers helped them to get a lease on a quarry near their new village. Working for themselves they found they could make enough money to build a school for their children. Trees and crops were planted around the village, but more importantly, dreams were growing. Freed from bondage, the villagers blossomed as individuals, each with a special dream of the future. They all agreed on a name for the new village: Freedom.

Working with Sankalp, the ex-slaves were able to get access to jobs, education, health care and a chance to participate in the political process. When the local elections were called in 2005, the people of Freedom Village surprised even the Sankalp workers. Across the area, ninety-nine recently freed slaves ran for office and seventy-nine of them won their campaigns. Even more amazing, in a society in which women are pushed into second-class status, thirty-one of the newly elected officials were women.

Sankalp has begun training for these seventy-nine newly elected leaders, some of whom need basic literacy skills. The freed slaves of Freedom Village are organizing with other communities. Many have used their government-awarded compensation money to buy a cow or two, and groups in each village have joined together to form a regional federation with more than 3,000 members. One part of the federation is a farmers' milk cooperative. With hundreds of milk producers working together, they have bargaining power and are able to get a higher price for their milk.

This federation of ex-slave communities is also having a profound impact on the natural environment. The slaveholders destroyed the national forests to strip-mine and the villagers are replanting the forests. Free the Slaves helped Sankalp and the villagers raise the needed funds, and now more than 10,000 trees have been planted. And these are not just any trees: the villagers are planting the five species of trees that Mahatma Gandhi recommended for village prosperity — trees that supply food, fuel, fodder, fiber and building materials.

Whole villages are coming out of slavery. They are replanting forests; landscaping strip mines into watersheds, ponds and irrigation systems; building schools and clinics; stopping child trafficking and "slave-proofing" their villages. As freed slaves take up the job of mayor, start new businesses and build new lives, the powerful forces for freedom locked up in every slave are being unleashed.

proposals that freed slaves after the American Civil War needed "forty acres and a mule," Indian law provides an immediate payment to secure food and shelter for freed slaves, and then a larger payment to help them gain economic self-sufficiency. This payment is enough to buy livestock, possibly land, or other tools or equipment to make a living. When government officials can be persuaded to provide the legally mandated payments, freed families can achieve autonomy and citizenship. Sadly, such payments are not always forthcoming and anti-slavery groups have to act as advocates for freed slaves, pushing the government to keep its promises.

Despite the number of obstacles, there is reason for hope in India. Traditional forms of slavery are so common there that the slaves are often used in plain sight. This actually makes it easier to locate and reach out to slaves and help them find their way to freedom. There is potential for very large numbers to be freed in a relatively short time. NGOs working to free slaves trapped in debt bondage have demonstrated this, and with limited resources thousands of families have been freed. One of these organizations is Sankalp, a partner of the American anti-slavery NGO Free the Slaves (see pages 73-74). Sankalp helps communities trapped in debt bondage to stand up and free themselves.

Ending slavery in India requires improving law enforcement, reducing corruption, addressing the factors that support slavery, such as poverty, and helping freed slaves to achieve their independence. While India may have the largest total number of slaves in the world, it is a rapidly growing country with a buoyant economy. The relatively small proportion of its population of 1 billion that is in slavery is acting as a drag on its economic growth, and is alienating potential trading partners abroad. For India, ending slavery is possible.

The United States

In the United States, the "land of the free," an estimated 17,000 men, women and children are trafficked and forced into slavery each year.[16] The vast majority of these people are tricked into being trafficked into the US, hoping for a job and a chance for a better life in one of the most prosperous nations in the world. These trafficking victims are trapped in slavery for varying lengths of time, but most are enslaved for between two and five years.

A conservative estimate of the number of people in slavery in the United States at any given time is 50,000, a staggering figure for any country. The work of these slaves generates millions of dollars in profits for traffickers and slaveholders. Trafficking rings and slavery operations have been found in as many as ninety cities, in nearly all fifty states and territories, with the largest number of cases concentrated in California, Florida, New York and Texas.[17]

The slaves in the US come from all over the world: Eastern Europe, Africa, Asia, Latin America and South Korea, but the majority come from China and Mexico. Many trafficking victims are brought to the US by traffickers who are the same nationality as the victims or who share a similar ethnic background. The work that

Sing Your Way to Slavery

Given Kachepa was born in Kalingalinga, Zambia, where he was one of six children. His mother died when he was six and his father died when he was eight. Along with his brothers and sisters, he moved in with his aunt, who also had six children. As a ten-year-old, Given began to sing in his local church choir and, strangely, it was this that led to his enslavement.

A charity group from Texas called Teaching Teachers to Teach (TTT) had started to help build schools in Zambia. When some of the TTT staff heard Given's boys' choir perform, they were impressed with the beauty of the boys' voices and the rich sound they made singing a capella, that is, without any instrumental accompaniment. In 1998 one couple from TTT decided to bring the choir to the United States and put on concerts to raise funds for building schools in Zambia. They were right about the choir; in the US people were willing to pay a lot of money to go to the concerts and made large donations to the charity. Sadly, the money proved too great a temptation. Instead of sending money back to the boys' families and building schools, the couple began to keep the money and to demand more and more work from the boys.

Given, at eleven, was the youngest member in the choir. The rosy promises made to the choirboys before they left home turned into a nightmare. For a year and a half the boys were made to give three to five concerts a day. If they were tired or sick, they were threatened. When not singing they were made to dig a hole for the couple's swimming pool. The boys were housed in a trailer and if they complained, their "boss" would cut off the gas so that they couldn't cook. Denied any medical care, several of the boys became seriously ill. (When they were later freed and given medical checkups, three of the boys tested positive for tuberculosis.)

The boys kept singing in the hope that some of the funds collected were being sent home to ease the poverty of their families. After more than a year of bad treatment, they realized that no money had been sent home to their families and they began to resist their boss, who quickly moved to deport the three oldest boys. His crime unraveled when US immigration officials began to question the boys. At first it was hard for officials to believe that a choir had been caught up in human trafficking and exploited to make money for the traffickers by singing in churches, but as the facts mounted, the boys were freed in 2000, cared for by volunteer families and given a chance to stay in the US.

Given now lives with a foster family in Texas, attends college, and speaks out against human trafficking whenever he can. When asked how he survived his enslavement, Given said,

> I had to stay focused and know what I believed in. There will always be people who will try to make you feel you are not worth anything, so you have to know your own worth. Having to sing like that many times, and missing my family, I had to stick it out and I knew that God would be there for me in the end. I was eleven when I came over. It was hard. Before I left, my brothers were trying to take care of me. They said they didn't want me to come, but I was thinking I could help my family and help myself and other people back home too, those that didn't have the opportunity to go to school.

Today Given Kachepa does just that, raising funds to help build schools in his native Zambia.

slaves do in the US roughly breaks down in this way: 50 percent work in prostitution, 30 percent in domestic service, 10 percent in agriculture, 5 percent in sweatshops, and 4 percent in restaurants.[18] Most of these employment sectors lack basic employee protections, especially the domestic sector. The majority of the instances of slavery in sweatshops occur in outlying American territories, such as Saipan and American Samoa, where there are few labor restrictions and where companies can claim that their products were "Made in the USA." The remaining 1 percent includes cases of slavery in the entertainment industry, cases of mail-order brides and the experience of Given Kachepa, described in the box opposite.

Luckily for Given, alert immigration officials realized that something was not right, which led to the boys' freedom. However, many law enforcement officials in the US have not received training in how to recognize trafficking victims and slaves. Less than 1 percent of slavery and trafficking cases result in prosecutions in the US, versus 70 percent for murders, as noted earlier.

New laws allow trafficking victims to stay safely in the US, but reform of immigration rules are still needed. The US has crafted one especially good new law against slavery. In 2000, Congress passed the Trafficking Victims Protection Act (TVPA). The TVPA:

- added the crimes of human trafficking, sex trafficking, forced labor and document servitude (the confiscation of passports and other documents as part of the trafficking scheme) to existing law;

- allocated temporary immigration status to victims of "severe forms of trafficking," such as minors trafficked into prostitution;
- created a special visa (the T-visa) for trafficking victims willing to testify against their traffickers, even if the case never makes it to court;
- allows for the protection of trafficking victims and for family members to be reunited with the victim in the US;
- provides for housing, psychological counseling, legal benefits and other social service needs of victims;
- established mandatory restitution for victims and allows victims to sue for damages in civil court; and
- established in 2001 the Office to Monitor and Combat Trafficking in Persons, otherwise known as the TIP Office, within the State Department.

There is still much for the US to do to get its trafficking problem under control, but the TVPA is a good first step. Since the law was passed, the number of arrests and convictions has doubled almost every year. The use of diplomacy through the Office to Monitor and Combat Trafficking in the State Department has led to new anti-slavery and anti-trafficking laws being passed in a number of countries. Overall, the report card for the US is mixed; while moving in the right direction, it fails on a number of measures: First, it has a number of laws on the books, particularly those concerning the importation of slave-made goods, which are rarely enforced due to a lack of personnel and funding. Second, as a crime of labor exploitation, anti-slavery work is stymied by the fact that there are far too few labor inspectors, especially in areas like southern Florida, where there is slavery in agriculture. Third, while diplomacy at low levels has had excellent results, ending slavery has not been made a high priority by any administration. Overall, the US is a world leader in anti-slavery expenditures and legislation, but it fails to deliver more than a fraction of its potential.

Chapter 5
Slavery and Globalization

All of us support and profit from slavery in some way, even if we don't mean to or don't realize it. The phenomenon of globalization means that the goods we buy are increasingly assembled in different parts of the world, using components from all over the world. There are many steps and parts that go into making a product, and slavery can creep into any one of them. This is true of lots of the things we buy: electronics, cars, clothing, food, jewelry and furniture. Slavery also creeps into investments. Pension funds or mutual funds may have stock, which is part ownership, in companies that employ other companies that use slave labor. Some of the steel in your car may have been made using pig iron or charcoal that was produced by slaves in Brazil. Similarly, a handful of the sugar in the jar at home may have come from sugar cane harvested by slaves in the Dominican Republic. Slavery infiltrates our lives through increasingly global markets.

Many people today don't notice globalization, but it is all around us. Our easy movement around the globe and cyberspace, the way we can phone almost anyone in almost any country, the way we are able to get news of what is happening almost everywhere all the time — all of these things point to a globalized world. Globalization transcends nation-state boundaries, meaning that ideas, foodstuffs, products, music, just about anything from a particular country or culture can be spread all over the planet. Globalization expert Martin Albrow describes this phenomenon as "the active dissemination of practices, values, technology and other human products throughout the globe," as well as the social and political changes that result from this process.[1]

Slavery and the World Economy

The most immediate and dramatic impact of globalization has been in the world economy. For centuries countries had controlled the flow of money across their borders, but in the mid-1980s these restrictions ended all at once for most countries. This meant that money could fly around the globe. With the touch of a button, businesses could hire or fire workers, buy, sell, or more likely, rent factories, and invest or divert funds. Businesses could move quickly whenever and wherever they found cheaper workers, and if there was a better, cheaper factory to rent somewhere else, then the business could just walk away from its current location.

Throughout history slavery has adapted fluidly to a changing world, and it continues to do so today. In terms of the world economy the global slave "business" is not worth much. One estimate states that all the work done by slaves in the whole world in a year is worth about $13 billion,[2] which is the same amount that spam emails cost the commercial world each year.[3] A study conducted by the United Nations in 2005 estimated that the global profits from human trafficking were about $31 billion a year.[4] This sounds like a lot of money, and it is, but consider that Americans throw away $31 billion dollars' worth of uneaten food each year.[5] In the global economy, these are small drops in a large ocean.

The low totals for the annual monetary return on slave work reflects two things: first that slaves tend to be used in low-value work, like quarrying and agriculture; and second, that their part in the global economy is very small. While slaveholders make a high rate of profit, there may only be 5 to 8 million slaveholders in the world, each holding, on average, a small handful of slaves.

The fact that slaves are very inexpensive everywhere on earth also tends to make slavery more alike everywhere on earth. With slavery illegal in every country, all slaveholders have to act in similar ways, hiding their slaves and squeezing out their profits. For the criminals who use slaves, this is not a problem. Criminals are very good at adapting to new situations; they have to be, because if they aren't, they get arrested or wiped out by the competition. Locked into a global economy, that means that money, goods and people flow in many directions; slave traffickers and slaveholders increasingly run their "businesses" in similar ways.

Two of the key themes of globalization are that businesses get spread around the planet and that governments have less and less control over these global businesses. These themes apply whether the businesses are legal or illegal or a mix of the two. New forms of slavery are spreading both slaves and slave-based activities around the globe with little government control. In Brazil, slaves are recruited in densely populated, economically depressed regions and then shipped over 1,600 kilometers (1,000 miles) to the forests where they make charcoal. The charcoal, in turn, is shipped another 1,600 kilometers (1,000 miles) for use in steel mills. The resulting steel is sold to Canada and the US. Women are trafficked from Burma or Laos for use in brothels in Thailand, Japan or Europe. Capital from Hong Kong funds the brothels of Thailand, and investment from Europe supports the charcoal operations of Brazil. Slaves from West Africa are found in Paris and New York; slaves from the Philippines are found in Vancouver and Saudi Arabia; and Eastern Europeans, especially women, are being dispersed as slaves all around the globe. Slavery is truly a globalized business.

With the financial systems of globalization, slave profits also flow smoothly across national borders. Governments find it very difficult, if not impossible, to stop the flow of this money. A country's laws stop at its border, but the global slave traffic flows over and under borders like water through a sieve. Many human traffickers operate over the Internet, using its global reach to find customers and make deals. All of this points to the importance and the difficulty of national governments learning to cooperate to fight international slavery.

Slavery and the Consumer

Removing products made by slave labor from our homes and lives is a new and special challenge. Most of the goods slaves make flow into their local economy, not into the international markets that lead into our homes. Millions of slaves in India, for example, grow food, quarry stone or produce other commodities that are used in their own towns and villages, never leaving the country. But there are also slaves in India and elsewhere, such as the children enslaved to weave carpets by hand, whose work feeds directly into the markets of Europe, North America and the rest of the world.

The huge demand for shrimp in the US and other rich countries has generated a gold rush along the coastlines of the developing world. From India to Bangladesh, from Indonesia to Ecuador, Guatemala and Brazil, coastal forests, mangrove swamps and natural beaches are ripped up to build hundreds of thousands of acres of shrimp farms. In all of these places adults and children are enslaved to cultivate and harvest the shrimp.[6] In some cases whole families are caught in debt bondage slavery, in others children are kidnapped and hustled off to shrimp and fish farms on remote islands. Children are regularly enslaved in fishing and shrimping, since kids can do the work and they are easier to enslave and control.

The special challenge of removing slave labor from products is based on the fact that today, slave-made commodities make up a very small and usually hidden part of the goods we buy. In the early nineteenth century it was

Why Boycotts Won't Work

It is repulsive to think about eating or wearing something made by slaves. No one ever wants to support slavery by buying slave-made goods. When we learn that we might be using products made by slaves, our first impulse is to stop buying those products and boycott the stores that sold them. In fact, a boycott can actually make things worse.

Take the example of cotton. In countries in Asia and Africa there are maybe two farmers out of a hundred who use slaves to grow cotton. If consumers boycott cotton from India or Africa, then what happens? First, the farmers who don't use slaves, who make lower profits, will be the hardest hit by the boycott. It is possible that these "free" farmers may lose their farms, in which case their children will have to leave school to find work, and their families may even become vulnerable to being enslaved through debt bondage. Second, the farmers who use slaves will be better able to survive the boycott since they have been making bigger profits, and they have another resource to fall back on, their slaves. Their slaves can be put to work at other jobs (denying those jobs to free workers) or even sold. The boycott may hurt the slaveholder, but it will hurt the free farmer much more.

easy to assume that if cotton came from the American South, slaves would have grown most of it. Likewise, in 1895, slaves harvested virtually all the rubber exported from the Congo to Europe.

Today the amount of slavery in any commodity is small. Cocoa is a good example. In the Ivory Coast there are about 800,000 farms that grow cocoa. No one knows for certain how many of these farms use slaves, but a good estimate is that it is less than 5 percent. This means that for every five farmers using slaves, there are ninety-five farmers who are not. When the farmers sell their cocoa to wholesalers, the small amount of slave-grown cocoa gets mixed up with the "free" cocoa, and there is no way to tell them apart. When the cocoa is exported from Ivory Coast to Europe and North America to be made into chocolate, it is mixed with cocoa from other countries and it becomes even harder to know what fraction is tainted with slavery.

The same problem applies to many other commodities. Cotton is grown with slave labor on three continents, but slave-grown cotton is just a tiny fraction of all the cotton grown worldwide. Coffee is also sometimes grown with slave labor and some sugar is harvested using slaves. Canada and the United States import large amounts of steel from Brazil and part of that steel has been made using slave-produced pig iron and charcoal. In the Congo, armed gangs force local villagers to dig a mineral called tantalum. The gangs sell the tantalum to exporters who send it to Europe and Asia for use in the production of cell phones and computers. The same situation applies to slaves who are made to weave cloth and rugs, make cigarettes, work in the fishing industry and make jewelry. The products they make get mixed in with the clothing, rugs, cigarettes, fish and jewelry produced by free workers. The special challenge is to take the slave labor out of the products without hurting the free farmers and workers at the same time.

Rugmark Rescues Raju

Raju is the youngest child ever to have been found weaving as a bonded laborer by Rugmark inspectors in India. He was rescued in 2000 and enrolled in the Balashrya Center for Bonded Laborers. At the age of seven, Raju was sold into bondage by his parents, who could not afford to take care of him; they felt that at least he would have the meals that his master would provide. The sum they received from the carpet loom owner was about $50. After weaving carpets day in and day out for the better part of a year, Raju was rescued by Rugmark inspectors. While signs of malnourishment are still present on his face, Raju's most prominent features are his sparkling eyes and smile. He enjoys learning Hindi, English, math, music and science at the Rugmark Center and stands out among his peers.

Before, Raju could not have dreamed of a life beyond a carpet loom shed. Now he wants to be a policeman when he grows up so that he can prevent other loom owners from forcing children to work.

Rugmark is an international charity that inspects and licenses carpet looms in India, Nepal and Pakistan. When carpet makers apply for a Rugmark license, they promise not to employ children under fourteen years of age and to pay adult weavers a minimum wage. In family carpet businesses, regular school attendance is required for children employed as helpers and only the loom-owner's children are permitted to work. Carpet makers promise to allow Rugmark's inspectors to examine their looms and workers at any time. The inspectors carry out random checks to see that the rules are being followed. Their license permits the carpet makers to put a Rugmark label, with a unique serial number, on their carpets so that every carpet can be traced all the way back to the loom.

Companies that import carpets to Europe and America pay at least 1 percent of the cost of the carpet to Rugmark. This money pays for schools and rehabilitation programs for children who have been freed from slavery in the carpet industry. In this way the former child slaves are safeguarded against being caught and enslaved again. To date, hundreds of child slaves have been freed and rehabilitated by Rugmark.

Getting Slavery Out of Our Lives

So how do we work to get slavery out of our lives? The best approach is to fight slavery where it is actually happening. That means stopping slavery on the farm, in the mine or in the workshop. To do that, everyone along the supply chain, from the farmer to the consumer, has to take some of the responsibility. A cotton T-shirt, for example, goes through many steps before it reaches the shop: harvested cotton goes from the farm to a cotton buyer; then to a cotton gin; raw cotton from the gin goes to a factory to be spun into thread; the thread goes to another factory to be woven into cloth; and the cloth is then shipped to be made into clothing. After the clothing is packaged, it is shipped to wholesalers; the wholesalers sell it to retailers; the retailers send it to shops where consumers buy it and take it home. Many of the steps along this supply chain take place in different countries, depending on where the T-shirt company and its subcontractors locate their factories. Everyone at every step along the chain can decide that they won't allow slavery in their product. If they agree to work together, it becomes much easier to send anti-slavery workers to the farms or garment factories where the slaves are being exploited.

A good example of this method is the Rugmark Foundation. The foundation inspects carpet looms in South Asia and labels rugs to guarantee they are not made with slave or child labor. With a labeling program, everyone along the supply chain knows that no slave labor was involved in creating the product (see page 89).

But how can we deal with slavery in the context of a commodity like cocoa? Clearly, it is not possible to put a label on every cocoa bean. The Cocoa Protocol, established in 2001, is a breakthrough in anti-slavery work. Organized by a US senator and congressman, it brings together the global chocolate industry, several anti-slavery and anti-child labor groups, labor unions and the International Labor Organization. Covering all cocoa-growing regions worldwide, the protocol acts as a treaty between all the groups, including consumers. It supports research and has established a foundation, the International Cocoa Initiative, which seeks to remove children and slaves from cocoa production and provide them with a safety net. In pilot communities, children are doing much less dangerous work and many are being sent to school. Research is still being conducted to find the best way to certify that cocoa from a country is free from slavery and child labor. Commodities like cotton, coffee, sugar and tantalum would also benefit from this sort of approach.

Another way to eliminate slave labor from the goods we buy is to buy Fair Trade products. Within the Fair Trade system, farmers are guaranteed a price for their crops that allows them to live decent lives and send their children to school. Once a farm has been certified as having no slavery or child labor, and as farming in an environmentally friendly way (some farmers also seek to be certified as organic producers), the farmer can sell his or her crops to the Fair Trade buyers. The price is not set by the world market, but rather by what would provide a

Fair Trade Resources

The best way to know that you are not buying something produced with slave labor is to buy Fair Trade or certified organic products whenever possible. While organic certification does not usually involve examining labor practices, the regular inspections by outsiders make it unlikely that child or slave labor is used. Here is a list of web resources to help you be an ethical consumer:

www.transfairusa.org
Here you can purchase Fair Trade products, learn more about these products and find stores in your area that sell them.

www.globalexchange.org
Global Exchange is an international human rights organization dedicated to promoting environmental, political and social justice. You can purchase slave labor–free products, including food, housewares, toys, clothing and jewelry.

www.americanapparel.net
American Apparel is a clothing company based in Los Angeles that has a vertically integrated supply chain — meaning that all the steps in producing the product are taken in the same place by the same company. This eliminates slavery from creeping into the supply chain at some point. The clothes are trendy, reasonably priced and many are available in certified organic cotton.

www.rugmark.org
This carpet-labeling charity certifies that carpets carrying its label are free from slave labor. A list of stores that sell these carpets is available on Rugmark's website.

decent life for the farmer and his or her family. Fair Trade buyers distribute the products to wholesalers and retailers where consumers can purchase them. The price of Fair Trade goods is normally a little higher than for goods that are not guaranteed to be free of slave labor or environmental abuse. Yet as the demand for Fair Trade goods increases, the supply will go up and the price will come down, though never so low as to threaten the livelihood of the farmers. Outside the Fair Trade system, farmers are hostages to a global market in commodities that can see the price of their crops move wildly up or down, with disastrous results. Products from more than forty countries are available from Fair Trade: chocolate, sugar, coffee and tea, as well as honey, cereals, rice, vanilla, flowers, wine, bananas and other fruits.

The Positive Side of Globalization

One of the major outcomes of globalization has been the rapid growth in the number, strength and influence of NGOs. Today it is hard to imagine a world without Greenpeace or Amnesty International or any of the thousands of other organizations that represent and act on our strongly held beliefs. Although anti-slavery groups were the very first human rights organizations to emerge, in the late eighteenth century, the vast majority of these groups were born in the last fifty years and have taken off with globalization.

The aim of anti-slavery organizations is to stop a crime that crosses boundaries, and their potential "market" of supporters and activists is the world population.

Their challenge is to get people to agree and to take action to end slavery, not locally but globally. Like governments, human rights organizations used to operate mainly inside national borders. With globalization, they quickly began to build partnerships and coalitions around the world. Multinational businesses and international organized crime were doing the same, but in the long run human rights organizations have one important advantage. International businesses and criminal groups are always trying to make the greatest profit, which means they must compete with other businesses and gangs. Especially in the world of organized crime, that competition can be deadly for the loser. Human rights groups sometimes have to compete, for supporters or for grant money. However, the important difference is that their ultimate goal is not profit but changing the world. Their readiness for global cooperation instead of competition gives anti-slavery organizations a long-term advantage: no time is wasted fighting other groups. Even if different organizations decide to take different approaches, the power and influence of human rights organizations has been increasing and will continue to increase.

NGOs have many advantages over governments in a globalized world. The structures of most of our governments were designed and set up in the eighteenth and nineteenth centuries, and they are sometimes slow to keep up with the speed of the twenty-first century. Rapid change means choices need to be made quickly, but our democracies require that the legislative branch make most decisions, in a process that is usually time-consuming. Normally, citizens can't participate directly in the process by voting on particular issues; they only participate by electing their representatives every few years. NGOs allow people to act more quickly on the issues that are most important to them, by volunteering, making donations or responding to urgent action requests. That is why a lot of people in democracies now spend more time and effort supporting NGOs than political parties. One of the clear outcomes of the globalization process has been this change: many people around the world and across borders are finding that they have more in common with each other on human rights issues than they have in common with their own governments. This is the globalization of our common belief in human rights, and it is ultimately more powerful than any multinational business or government.

Chapter 6
Controversies and Problems

There are many sides to every issue, and slavery is no exception. Even when it comes to an issue as universally opposed as slavery, there are disagreements, problems and controversies. With contemporary slavery, controversies exist over the methods used to bring slaves to freedom and the role of slavery in prostitution. There are numerous obstacles and problems faced by those working to eradicate slavery, including a lack of knowledge of the issue and a lack of funds to combat slavery. Slaves themselves face myriad problems once they are freed. A better understanding of the problems and controversies is needed before any of them can be brought to a resolution.

Controversy One: Redemption

Redemption is the practice of purchasing slaves in order to free them. Proponents of redemption believe that buying slaves is the fastest and safest way to bring them to freedom. Opponents maintain that buying slaves creates a market for slaves, generates profits for the slaveholders and does not lead to the end of slavery — if anything it perpetuates the practice. The controversy over redemption is not new; it has been debated on and off for hundreds of years. In fact, as long as there have been slaves there have been people willing to buy them their freedom. This practice existed in ancient Greece, Rome and other early civilizations. During wars throughout history, enemies were captured, enslaved and then ransomed — a strategy that helped to finance the wars. Redemption was widespread in the US during the era when slavery flourished; the abolitionist Frederick Douglass was himself a redeemed slave.

The issue of redemption came to the public's attention in the 1990s when groups like Christian Solidarity International started buying slaves in war-torn Sudan. As international focus has shifted to the genocide taking place in the Darfur region of Sudan, the issue of slave redemption in Sudan has faded, but redemption remains a controversial way to address slavery in places where local law enforcement cannot be relied on to arrest slaveholders and to free slaves.

Redemption, in some cases, is thought to do more harm than good. Many people consider it complicity in a crime. They argue that slavery is illegal everywhere and freedom is a fundamental human right that shouldn't have to be purchased. To use an analogy, if your iPod was stolen, you wouldn't feel you should buy it back from the thief — that would be rewarding criminal behavior. In the same way, buying slaves from slaveholders in order to free them rewards the slaveholders' criminal activity. In Sudan in the 1990s, redemption may actually have helped to perpetuate the slavery the redeemers were trying to stop. Profits made from the sale of slaves to foreigners (who then freed them) went to buy more weapons, fueling the civil war that led to more people being captured and enslaved.

The best way to think about redemption is as a last option. When people are enslaved, everything needs to be done to win their freedom, even if it includes buying their freedom. While there are costs to redemption, the cost of slavery is too high to rule out redemption in situations where no other options exist for winning freedom for slaves. Slave redemption does have a role in the fight against slavery, but it should be viewed as the lesser of two evils, where the greater evil is slavery. All other options should be exhausted before choosing the course of redemption. However, in situations where there is nothing else to do, where the government and police stand by and let people suffer in slavery that endangers their lives, little doubt remains about whether redemption should be practiced.

Controversy Two: Prostitution and Slavery

Slaves everywhere are frequently sexually abused, raped and forced into prostitution. This is one thing that female slaves have suffered throughout history and still suffer — vulnerability to being sexually assaulted and exploited. Today, slaves are forced into prostitution in many places, including in Europe and North America. A large number of all human trafficking victims — 43 percent according to the International Labor Organization

— are forced into prostitution in a process known as sex trafficking. Sex trafficking is so commonly reported in the media that many people believe all human trafficking is aimed at enslavement in prostitution.

There have always been ties between slavery and prostitution, so the link between them is not controversial. The controversy that has erupted is whether *all* prostitution is slavery and centers on the question of whether women can truly *choose* to engage in prostitution.

On one side of this issue are people and groups, primarily women's groups, who believe that prostitution is a form of slavery, and that all women who sell sex are slaves, and that prostitution, like slavery, needs to be abolished. They argue that all prostitution is forced in some way, either by violence or by social or economic pressures, and that no person would freely choose to become a prostitute. According to this view, even if a woman chooses to engage in prostitution, she is not exercising free will because society and the need she has to care for herself and her family have severely limited her options.

Those on the other side of this controversy contend that some, but not all, prostitution is slavery. This side argues that it is unfortunate that people end up in situations where one of their remaining options is to work in the sex trade, but it is not a choice that should be restricted, they say, especially when women can exercise control over their work in prostitution. Advocates of this view say sex workers should have greater protection in their work and some even promote the legalization of prostitution.

There are several points to the legalization argument. First, if the government is in control of prostitution, it can regulate and oversee the business. Second, if prostitution is legalized, it comes out of the shadows and into the open. In this situation, sex workers can exercise greater control over their working lives and can go to the police if necessary without fear of punishment. The legalization of prostitution, to those on this side of the debate, lessens many of the dangerous aspects of work in the sex trade and makes cases of forced prostitution more readily identifiable.

Those on the other side of the argument point to places where prostitution is legal, such as Germany and the Netherlands, and they argue that this only creates a situation in which criminals can more easily operate and that it increases the number of women caught up in prostitution. Since legalization often includes taxation, they point to the morally questionable fact of governments being supported by commercial and potentially exploited sex workers.

There is some agreement between the two sides of this debate. Everyone agrees that nonconsensual or forced prostitution is slavery and must be stopped. Everyone agrees that no minors should engage in prostitution. Both sides feel a sense of urgency and believe that prostitution in its current form is only hurting the women involved. But as long as these two groups are in conflict, some of their energy and resources will go toward opposing each other rather than helping people who are caught in terribly abusive situations.

Both sides of this debate are carefully watching the outcome of a new law in Sweden, where prostitution was previously legal. The new law leaves the *sale* of sex as legal; it is the *purchase* that is made illegal. By criminalizing only the purchase of sex, the Swedes are attempting to redress the imbalance of power between men and women. In passing the law, the Swedish parliament viewed the economic and social relationship between a woman selling sex and a man buying sex as a very unequal one, and it held that men's ability to buy women's bodies could be seen as a form of male dominance to be resisted and controlled.

This approach is unique and runs counter to recent laws in Germany and Holland that attempt to reduce the demand for women trafficked into prostitution by legalizing and regulating brothels. Sweden is trying to extinguish the demand for prostitution (and trafficked people) at the point of consumption. Germany and Holland are instead trying to reduce the number of enslaved prostitutes in the supply chain by arresting traffickers. Do either of these approaches work? At this point, no one knows for certain. Criticism has been leveled at the Swedish law for pushing prostitution underground and increasing the number of trafficking victims, but there is as yet no evidence to support this. The Swedish government states that the law is reducing the number of women exploited in prostitution, but again little evidence is available. The legalization of brothels in the state of Queensland, Australia, has been interpreted as both decreasing trafficking by some commentators and increasing it by others. Given that the demand for prostitution is often met with women (and children) who have been trafficked, it is critical that detailed and unbiased research be carried out as quickly as possible.

Problem One: Lack of Awareness and Resources

A global campaign could eradicate global slavery, but the problems of a general lack of awareness and resources stand in the way. Awareness is growing, but people in many countries still find it hard to believe that slavery exists today. This is in part because the number of slaves — 27 million — is both the largest number of slaves at any one time in history and the smallest proportion of the world's population ever enslaved. When slavery grew after World War II, it grew as an illegal activity and in such a way that few people noticed what was going on.

Increasing awareness is a tough challenge. Anti-slavery groups need to raise money so that they can tell people about modern slavery, but until people know about slavery they won't help by contributing money. Put simply, you need resources to raise awareness and you have to raise awareness to get resources. Anti-slavery organizations are trying to break out of this circle, but they need the help of governments.

Unfortunately, slavery is not a top priority for any government today. Speeches are made and reports are issued, but governments are all talk and little or no action. Governments, especially powerful ones like the US and the European Union, have the ability and the funds to significantly reduce the amount of slavery in the world today. However, because of the low levels of public awareness of slavery, politicians won't make this a high priority. The United States, for example, spends about $200 million a year to fight human trafficking and slavery, which is about the same amount that it spends on water projects in North Dakota. Not including the war in Iraq, the US government spent $18.6 billion dollars on weapons and military aid for other countries in 2004[1] — and it spends about 1 percent of that amount fighting slavery. Around the world more slaves come to freedom through the work of anti-slavery groups than through government action. There are politicians who really want to change this, but there are others who haven't gotten the word yet. The important thing is that when governments really get involved big changes will happen. A good example is the dramatic increase in the number of rescued slaves in Brazil after the Lula government made the eradication of slavery a priority.

One of the most important areas needing resources is the training of police. In almost every country today, only the smallest number of police have been trained to identify slavery and trafficking and to use the most effective ways to investigate these crimes. Police officers often mistakenly view human trafficking victims as illegal aliens or criminals themselves. Governments need to make sure their police forces understand slavery and trafficking and are equipped to handle such cases.

Problem Two: The Complications of Freedom

Liberation is the beginning, not the end, of the process that leads to freedom. Some ex-slaves need very little to get on their feet, others will need a lifetime of support. It is absolutely crucial that ex-slaves don't just move from slavery into extreme poverty. There would be little point to liberation if the 27 million slaves in the world were simply pushed over to join the 1 billion destitute people in the world living on about a dollar a day. Around the world are examples of liberation that have gone well and cases that have been a disaster.

Perhaps no other country in the world demonstrates the consequences of a botched emancipation so dramatically as the United States. The US has suffered, and continues to suffer, from the injustices handed out to nearly 4 million ex-slaves following the Civil War. Generations of African Americans were sentenced to second-class status, exploited and abused. Without education and access to jobs, it was very difficult for African-American families to build lives that allowed full participation and well-being in American society. Today, victims of crimes receive restitution for what they have lost, for the damage they have suffered. But no such restitution has come for the stolen lives of millions of slaves.

If today's slavery were ended in the next fifty years, which is a real possibility, would we really want the next four, five or twenty generations to face the problems of emancipation gone wrong? Ending slavery should not create a population whose suffering and anger continues for years to come. In the world after slavery, a key question is: even if there is restitution, how can there be forgiveness?

Many people would say that slavery is a crime beyond forgiveness. It is no momentary crime, but brutality and exploitation that can stretch over generations. It combines the most horrible crimes known — torture, rape, kidnapping, murder and the destruction of the human mind and spirit. It is exploitation, injustice and violence all rolled together.

A common theme of nineteenth-century abolitionists was that the minds injured by slavery included the minds of the slaveholders. They argued that by dehumanizing another person in order to enslave them, the slaveholder dehumanized himself. It is hard to feel any concern for slaveholders, but many ex-slaves recognize the damage slavery does to the master. A community that allows slavery to exist is sick to its roots. For the ex-slave to become an autonomous citizen, that sickness needs to be treated. This is especially true because today many freed slaves live in the same area where they used to live as slaves. Ex-slaves and their slaveholders may see each other regularly. If injustices are not resolved, it will be impossible for either group to move on. In the US, the ugly sickness of slavery re-emerged as peonage and in segregation, discrimination and lynching. In part, this was because most Americans wanted to ignore the legacy of slavery. The needs of freed slaves were not met in the years following 1865, and ever since there has been an attempt to draw the curtain over the past, to let bygones be bygones.

The country of South Africa also faced this problem.

For decades the South African government enforced rules that made all nonwhites into second-class citizens. Nonwhites were excluded from schools, jobs, housing and treated with contempt and brutality. When this racist system called apartheid ended, South Africa had to face up to the horrific large-scale murders and torture of the past. Many South Africans argued that collective amnesia would best serve reconstruction. But one of the country's new leaders, Desmond Tutu, explained: "Our common experience in fact is the opposite — that the past, far from disappearing or lying down and being quiet, is embarrassingly persistent, and will return and haunt us unless it has been dealt with adequately. Unless we look the beast in the eye we will find that it returns to hold us hostage."[2] In the United States that beast has been on the prowl for more than 100 years and has evolved into new forms of discrimination and injustice. Putting down that beast is one of the country's greatest challenges. Ensuring that the same beast does not grow up when slaves are freed today is a challenge for the whole world.

Chapter 7
How We Will End Slavery

It may seem naive to assert that after more than 5,000 years of slavery, we will bring it to an end. Slavery has been a permanent part of human existence throughout all of human history, but like smallpox or the burning of witches, its time is over. Human slavery may seem the immovable monolith, but it is actually a weak shell ready to topple. There will be pockets of resistance to ending slavery. However, for most of the 27 million slaves in the world today, the transition to citizenship and restored dignity is not just immediately possible, it is inevitable.

Why Now?
There are a number of reasons why eradication is possible and a favorable social, political and economic context provides a foundation. This can be seen in four key challenges that we do *not* have to face. The first is that we do not have to win the moral argument against slavery; no government or organized interest group is pressing the case that slavery is desirable or even acceptable. No priest or minister is standing in the pulpit and giving biblical

justifications for slavery. No philosophers offer up rationalizations for slavery. In fact, with the exception of a handful of criminals, the world is united in its condemnation of slavery. The Universal Declaration of Human Rights simply underscores this, placing freedom from slavery at the top of the list of fundamental rights. The moral challenge today is how we can act effectively on our universally held belief in the absolute and essential equality of human dignity.

The second challenge that we do not have to face is the argument that slavery is necessary for our economic well-being. The actual monetary value of slavery in the world economy is extremely small, a tiny fraction of the global economy. The end of slavery does not threaten the livelihood of any country or industry. No country can say, "We would like to end slavery, but we just can't afford it." In fact, the opposite is true. While slaves may make money for slaveholders, they are a drag on a country's economy. They contribute little to national production; their work is concentrated on the lowest rung of the economic ladder, as they have low-skill jobs that are dirty and dangerous. Slaves work both ineffectively and as little as they can, and who can blame them? The value of their work is stolen and pocketed by criminals. Economically, except for the criminals, slaves are a waste. They contribute next to nothing to a country's economy; they buy nothing in a country's markets. They are an untapped economic resource.

In Northern India models of community-based liberation and economic reintegration are being tested and polished. In more than 100 villages, the story is the same: with only a little assistance, freed slaves dramatically increase their incomes, choose to invest immediately in education for their children, increase their food consumption and improve their health, and buy assets that provide a livelihood for their families, such as land and livestock. For poor countries with high levels of slavery, significantly increasing the earning and spending of ex-slaves would be a small but important improvement in the national economy. At the international level, if you compare countries on the strength of their economies and how many slaves they have, the picture is clear — the more slaves, the weaker the economy. There is simply no economic reason to keep slavery alive.

The third great challenge we do not have to face is the need to pass laws against slavery. For the most part, the laws needed to end slavery are already on the books. Around the world, some of these laws need updating and expanding and some need harsher penalties increased, but nowhere on earth is slavery legal. The challenge today is to get governments to enforce the laws that they already have. That can be difficult when there is corruption, but most citizens are ready to resist corruption and to stop slavery. In the last few years, the governments of Ghana, Oman, Japan and the United Arab Emirates have all been pressed by their own citizens and other countries to enforce and improve their anti-slavery laws. This can be a slow process, especially in a poor country, but when it is done successfully, it is one of the most effective ways to stop slavery.

There is a lack of funding to train police in the use of anti-slavery laws. And given the international nature of human trafficking, nearly all these laws need to be brought into harmony with one another. The most important laws that need to be enacted are those that involve appropriating the necessary government funds for eradication.

The fourth reason that it is now easier to end slavery is also the newest. In the past slavery was regularly linked to race and ethnicity. Whole populations of people were considered fair game for enslavement because they were a different color or belonged to a different tribe or ethnic group. Today there are still people who hold racist views, but they are a shrinking minority and they have to face up to some new powerful knowledge. In the past ten years, research into human genetics, especially the mapping of the human genome, has confirmed that concepts of race are biologically obsolete. Race as a collection of attributes that physically separates one group of human beings from another simply does not exist. The essential unity of all humans at the biological level is an established fact. People may still use race as a way to discriminate or segregate, but this only reflects their own prejudices, not any sort of true difference between people. The knowledge of the true unity of our human species means that one of the main excuses for slavery has been demolished.

The Cost of Ending Slavery

Debt bondage in South Asia accounts for as many as 10 million of the world's slaves. If we can end this form of slavery, millions of slaves will come to freedom. The good news is that the programs for liberation and reintegration in Northern India are well developed and well tested. If we go back over several years and add together the costs of paying the outreach workers, paying for their transportation to rural villages, organizing and guaranteeing seed money, maintaining microcredit unions, and keeping the local organization's office[1] running, then divide that sum by the number of families they help to freedom in a year, the result is about $150 per family.

So, for the price of a nice lunch or a pair of designer jeans, a family in India goes from slavery to freedom. None of that money goes to pay off the illegal debt that holds the family in bondage or to give money to criminals to "buy" the slave's freedom. What the price does include is the cost of helping the family achieve an independent life and getting their children to school. Freedom may be precious, but it doesn't have to be expensive.

Knowing what it will cost to end slavery in a country makes it possible to build an effective strategy for eradication with meaningful government participation. Remarkably, the balance of costs and benefits for ending slavery makes it a great investment. In Ghana anti-slavery groups have found that it costs about $400 to take a child out of slavery in the fishing industry, return him or her to their family, and help that family achieve economic stability.[2] If we use this higher figure as an estimate of what it will take to free all slaves, what would that mean in terms of the price of ending all slavery? Ending slavery on the planet for 27 million slaves would cost $10.8 billion. That amount of money is beyond the reach of human rights organizations, but it is 1 percent of the current annual budget of the British government or $328 for every person in Canada. Shared among the rich countries, the cost would be pennies per person. Freedom is not just affordable; it's a bargain.

These cost comparisons are important because they show that money is not the barrier to ending slavery. They demonstrate that with political will and a fairly small amount of input, eradication is achievable. Of course, it is true that freedom for many slaves will cost more than the $150 it costs to free a family found in Northern India or the $400 that it costs to remove a child from slavery in the fishing industry in Ghana. Helping people who have been trafficked into Europe and North America will be even more expensive. The cost involved in catching and punishing the human traffickers linked to organized criminal gangs will be even higher. These criminal networks are notoriously hard to crack. In many parts of the world, the poverty that increases a person's vulnerability to slavery is so acute that its root causes must be tackled. Then there are the governments that tacitly support slavery and exploit their own citizens as forced labor. Working with these unelected dictatorships will require enormous diplomatic and economic negotiation. But even if the cost of global freedom doubles or triples, it is still a relatively small sum, an infinitesimally small fraction of the global economy. And as we've seen, stable and sustainable freedom generates economic growth and, in a way, pays for itself.

Step by Step

The abolitionists of the past had the great benefit of a precise goal — passing a law to make slavery illegal. Ours — the eradication of slavery — is a much wider goal. While the basic conditions of slavery are fundamentally the same the world over, every slave lives and suffers in a unique situation. The social, cultural, political, economic and sometimes religious packaging that is wrapped around slavery in different countries and cultures means that our eradication methods need to follow general patterns that can then be adapted to each unique setting. While some slaves can be freed individually, in some cases whole communities need to be freed together to ensure a sustainable liberation.

One avenue leads us to think hard about the products that are tainted with slavery. But as we've seen, this problem can't normally be fixed at the point of purchase. To take the slave labor out of cotton or cocoa or any other product, we have to attack slavery at its source. It is much more effective to set slaves free and arrest the criminals who enslave them than it is to boycott goods that might be tainted with slavery. We also have to crack the system that feeds slavery into the product chain; otherwise criminals will just suck more people into slavery. Once they are freed, ex-slaves need support to build independent and stable lives. Here the circle closes and the way ahead becomes clearer. If you are worried about slavery in cotton, notice that the $150 you might spend on new clothes is also the cost of freeing a family enslaved in agriculture in Northern India. Don't stop buying clothes that might be made with slave-produced cotton, just start investing in freedom and urging businesses to join with consumers, NGOs and governments in ending slavery for good.

Using our role as consumers is just one way ahead. Starting at the grassroots level and working up, there are many more ways to stop slavery. In farms and villages some individuals are risking their lives to help others out of slavery. Local anti-slavery and human rights organizations support these workers. To increase their impact and free more slaves, at least three things need to happen. The first is that local anti-slavery workers need protection. Those who live in the rich Global North need to keep reminding governments that these anti-slavery heroes are the sharp end of the tool that breaks chains and that they deserve our support. The second thing needed at the grassroots level is the money to expand successful programs. Careful tracking shows efficient and powerful local programs on every continent, but most are limping along on a shoestring. Third, we need to increase the number of liberators. It is a perfectly reasonable goal to say, "Where there is one liberator today, there will be three next year." In spite of the danger, there is no shortage of people ready to do local anti-slavery work. It is simply a question of resources. We need to find the best anti-slavery workers and then invest in giving them apprentices and extending their reach and activity.

Supporting individual anti-slavery workers is not the way to end slavery for good, but it is the job that needs doing now. These liberators are like the emergency aid workers who fight epidemics. For every epidemic, research is needed; health policies have to change; the whole public health system of sewers, water treatment and hospitals needs to be rebuilt. But when people are starting to die *today*, someone needs to deliver the vaccine and the food *today*. Today there are slaves waiting to be freed. As we begin the long process of aligning governments with these goals and building the international alliance against slavery, grassroots workers are all that usually stands between slaves and a lifetime of slavery.

At the level of governments, two related and achievable actions are likely to take place in the next five to ten years, and lawmakers in many countries of the Global North are already preparing to move ahead. The first action is that rich countries should devote the necessary diplomatic and financial resources to make the end of slavery a priority. There are many carrots and a few sticks that might be offered to countries that continue to have high levels of slavery. The second action is that some of these resources should be directed to the Global South to support the enforcement of local laws against slavery and the establishment of sustainable lives for ex-slaves.

At the international level, existing patterns of research, policy, diplomacy and outreach can easily be transferred to ending slavery. We know that when governments really get involved in collective international efforts, big changes can happen. In 1988 the Global Polio Eradication Initiative began, with nearly every government in the world promising to take part. In that year, the crippling polio disease was active in 125 countries. By

Combating Slavery on the International Level

Major international prohibitions against slavery and forced labor include:

- League of Nations Slavery Convention of 1926
- ILO Forced Labor Convention (No. 29), 1930
- Universal Declaration of Human Rights, 1948
- Geneva Conventions, 1949
- United Nations Supplementary Convention on the Abolition of Slavery, the Slave Trade, and Institutions and Practices Similar to Slavery, 1956
- ILO Abolition of Forced Labor Convention (No. 105), 1957
- International Covenant on Civil and Political Rights, 1966
- International Covenant on Economic, Social and Cultural Rights, 1966
- ILO Worst Forms of Child Labor Convention (No. 182), 1999
- United Nations Convention against Transnational Organized Crime, 2000

2003, there were only six countries left with active polio. As with many diseases, it will be difficult to wipe out the polio virus completely, but millions of children and adults have been saved from being crippled. Slavery can also go from being global, pernicious and pervasive to being a rare crime.

We are all familiar with the role of UN weapons inspectors. Their job has been to ensure that countries keep the promises they have made when ratifying UN conventions on weapons of mass destruction. Given that essentially every country in the world has ratified the various UN anti-slavery conventions and that prohibitions against slavery have been ruled to be universal and fundamental by international courts, it is perfectly reasonable to establish UN slavery inspectors. Their job would be to help countries identify and correct holes in the enforcement of their own laws and their international commitments.

None of these steps require any radical new approaches or rules. Existing structures, tools and methods simply need to be turned to with sufficient focus and resources to push slavery into the waste bin with polio.

To ensure that freed slaves build new lives, to see that communities overcome the sickness of slavery, to find the best ways to liberate slaves and to help governments enforce their own anti-slavery laws means building a sound understanding of what slavery is today and discovering the best points of intervention. We cannot solve a problem we do not understand. If we really want to end slavery, we have to get past outrage and focus on analysis, then build practical tools and solutions from that analysis and commit to providing all the necessary resources to follow through. We stand at a moment in human history where our economies, governments, understanding and moral beliefs, as well as our hearts and minds, are aligned in a constellation that can bring slavery to an end.

Timeline

Slavery has been around for as long as humans have. It existed long before people started keeping records, using money and making laws.

c. 6800 BC The first city in the world develops in Mesopotamia. Warfare begins when people start to own land and technology develops. During war, enemies are captured and forced to work – the first instance of slavery.

c. 2575 BC Egyptians send slave-raiding expeditions down the Nile River to capture more slaves. Artwork in temples depicts slaves being captured during war.

c. 550 BC In Athens, the Greeks use approximately 30,000 slaves to work in the city-state's silver mines.

c. 70 BC Spartacus, a gladiator and slave and leader of an uprising of 120,000 slaves against the Roman Republic, dies (probably in battle, but his body is never found).

120 The Roman military captures thousands of slaves at a time during military campaigns. Half of the population of the city of Rome is estimated to be slaves.

c. 1000 In rural England, poor agricultural workers and their families are commonly held in debt bondage to wealthy landowners.

c. 1250 Between 5,000 and 25,000 slaves are taken from West Africa to the Mediterranean in the trans-Saharan slave trade, where they go on to be sold in Europe and the Middle East.

c. 1380 After the Black Plague, the slave trade in Europe starts again to address the labor shortage. The slaves are brought from Europe, the Middle East and North Africa.

c. 1444 The first slaves are brought to Europe from West Africa in the beginning of the Atlantic slave trade. When Europeans begin traveling to the Americas, the trade greatly expands. By the time the trade ends around 1870, approximately 13 million slaves captured from Africa have been taken to slavery in Europe and the Americas.

1619 Slavery in the American colonies begins, with the delivery of twenty Africans to the English settlement at Jamestown, Virginia.

1789 During the French Revolution, on August 26, the French National Assembly ratifies the Declaration of the Rights of Man, which states, "Men are born and remain free and equal in rights."

1791–1804 The slaves of Saint Domingue (now Haiti) revolt against French colonialists, finally winning their independence and their freedom from slavery.

1803 Denmark bans the African slave trade, becoming the first country in Europe to do so.

1807 The British Parliament bans British ships from transporting slaves and British colonies from importing slaves, after years of lobbying by abolitionists led by Thomas Clarkson.

1808 The United States ends the importation of Africans into the country as slaves. By this time there are approximately 1 million slaves in the US.

1814 The Netherlands officially ends Dutch participation in the African slave trade.

1820 Spain ends the slave trade in areas south of the Equator, but the trade continues in Cuba until 1888.

1825 Slavery is abolished in Argentina, Bolivia, Chile and Peru.

1833 August 23. The Slavery Abolition Act outlaws slavery in British colonies (including Canada).

1834 August 1. Slaves in all British colonies are finally freed. About $100 million is paid to slave owners in compensation for losses, but nothing is paid to slaves.

1840 The World Anti-Slavery Convention is held in London. Its purpose is to gather activists, help abolition efforts, and assist in areas where slaves have been freed.

1848 France abolishes slavery at home and in its colonies.

1850 Brazil ends its involvement in the slave trade.

1861 Alexander II, czar of Russia, emancipates all serfs in the country, numbering around 50 million.

1863 The Emancipation Proclamation, delivered by President Abraham Lincoln during the American Civil War, frees all slaves in the Confederate states.

1863 The Netherlands abolishes slavery in all its colonies.

1888 Brazil emancipates the 725,000 slaves in the country, ending slavery in South America.

1910 In Paris the International Convention for the Suppression of the White Slave Trade is signed, making it the first convention of its kind.

1915 The colony of Malaya abolishes slavery.

1923 Hong Kong bans the sale of young girls as domestic slaves.

1926 The Slavery Convention is passed by the League of Nations, obligating member countries to work to end all forms of slavery.

1926 Burma ends slavery.

1927 Sierra Leone officially abolishes slavery.

1936 The king of Saudi Arabia ends the importation of new slaves into the country and regulates the treatment of slaves already in the country, instead of abolishing slavery.

1938–1945 Thousands of Korean and Chinese women are forced to become sexual slaves in Japanese military "comfort stations," or brothels.

1939–1945 The Nazi government in Germany uses slavery in farming and industry. Approximately 9 million people are forced to work until they are unable to go on. They are then sent to concentration camps.

1948 The Universal Declaration of Human Rights is passed by the United Nations. It includes, in article 4, the assertion that "No one shall be held in slavery or servitude; slavery and the slave trade shall be prohibited in all their forms."

1952 Approximately 40,000 Japanese children are sold into sexual slavery in this year alone; brothel owners pay between $25 and $100 per child.

1954 China begins allowing prisoners to be used as laborers in the *laogai* prison camps.

1956 UN passes the Supplementary Convention on the Abolition of Slavery, the Slave Trade, and Institutions and Practices Similar to Slavery.

1962 Saudi Arabia and Yemen abolish slavery.

1974 Freed slaves in Mauritania begin the group called El Hor (meaning "freedom") to oppose slavery. Organization leaders believe that emancipation of slaves is impossible without the ability to enforce anti-slavery laws and a way to make sure former slaves can be economically independent.

1975 The United Nations establishes the Working Group on Contemporary Forms of Slavery. The group gathers information and makes recommendations about slavery around the world.

1976 Bonded labor is abolished in India.

1980 Mauritania bans slavery for the fourth time, though the situation does not change.

1989 The National Islamic Front gains control of the government in Sudan. Militias raid villages in the south of the country, capturing and enslaving citizens there.

1992 Pakistan ends indentured servitude and the *peshgi* (bonded money) system. The government does not adequately enforce the law.

1994 Anti-Slavery International shows evidence of slavery in Nepal to the United Nations.

1996 In Germany the Rugmark campaign begins. The Rugmark seal on a rug guarantees that no slave or child labor was used to produce it.

1997 A commission is created by the United Nations to investigate allegations of the enslavement of people by the Burmese (Myanmar) government. Investigators are refused entry into the country, but they are able to gather enough evidence to condemn the slavery there.

1997 The United States bans the importation of goods made by child bonded laborers.

1999 NGOs call for international aid and a ceasefire in Sudan, with the hope of ending slavery there.

1999 The International Labor Organization establishes international standards for protecting children from forced labor, prostitution and other harmful work in the Convention Against the Worst Forms of Child Labor.

1999 The Protocol to Prevent, Suppress, and Punish Trafficking in Persons, Especially Women and Children, supplementing the United Nations Convention against Transnational Organized Crime is signed. The protocol's purpose is to address trafficking in women and children and to promote cooperation between countries in that area.

2000 Nepal abolishes all forms of debt bondage.

2000 The US Congress passes the Trafficking Victims Protection Act. The act establishes that trafficking is a form of slavery, establishes the crime of human trafficking, and sets out benefits and protections for victims of trafficking.

2000 Free the Slaves is formed in the US as the American sister organization of Anti-Slavery International.

2001 *Slavery: A Global Investigation*, a documentary about slavery and forced child labor in the chocolate industry, is released. The film receives a Peabody Award and two Emmy Awards.

2002 Chocolate companies and NGOs sign the Cocoa Protocol, which ensures the end of slavery and child labor in the cocoa supply chain. NGOs, chocolate companies and local governments form the International Cocoa Initiative to enforce the protocol and monitor production.

2003 The United States enacts economic sanctions against Burma (Myanmar) for the government's use of forced labor.

2004 February 27 is declared National Anti-Slavery Day in many US states.

2005 The International Labor Organization publishes the first global report on forced labor.

2006 Actress Julia Ormond is appointed first UN Goodwill Ambassador for the Abolition of Slavery and Human Trafficking.

2006 The UN passes a Resolution on the Bicentennial Commemoration of the Abolition of the Slave Trade.

2007 The new democratic government of Mauritania presents to the international community a plan for the complete eradication of slavery in that country.

2008 A US labor group report shows that slavery in shrimp farms of Southeast Asia feeds into massive increases of shrimp to North America, and the sale of slave-tainted shrimp by most major retailers.

Notes

Chapter 1. The New Slavery

1. United Nations, *The World at Six Billion*, Report from the Population Division, Department of Economic and Social Affairs. www.un.org/esa/population/publications/sixbillion/sixbillion.htm.
2. Cam Simpson, "Pipeline to Peril," *Chicago Tribune*, October 9, 2005. www.chicagotribune.com/news/specials/chi-nepal-1-story,0,5497142.story.
3. The Narmada Bachao Andolan, "Supreme Court Directs M.P. Government to Provide Land-based Rehabilitation; Refuses to Stay SSP Construction Despite Incomplete Rehabilitation," press release, New Delhi, India, April 17, 2004.
4. Jeffrey Sachs, *The End of Poverty* (New York: Penguin, 2005), 59.
5. Brian Woods and Kate Blewitt, *Slavery: A Global Investigation*, documentary film, TrueVision Productions, September 2001.

Chapter 2. Slavery Throughout History

1. *Webster's New World College Dictionary*, 4th ed., 2004, 1347.
2. British Broadcasting Company, "Focus on the Slave Trade," September 3, 2001. http://news.bbc.co.uk/1/hi/world/africa/1523100.stm.
3. David Brion Davis, *Inhuman Bondage: The Rise and Fall of Slavery in the New World* (New York: Oxford University Press, 2006), 124, 128.
4. Harriet Beecher Stowe Center. *Harriet Beecher Stowe's Life & Time.* www.harrietbeecherstowecenter.org/life/#war.

5. Adam Hochschild, *King Leopold's Ghost* (New York: Houghton Mifflin, 1998), 233.
6. US Department of State, *Trafficking in Persons Report* (June 2006), 268.

Chapter 3. Types of Slavery

1. United Nations. Convention against Transnational Organized Crime, Protocol to Prevent, Suppress and Punish Trafficking in Persons, Especially Women and Children. Protocol Art. 3.a-b. www.unodc.org/pdf/crime/a_res_55/res5525e.pdf.
2. United Nations. Convention against Transnational Organized Crime, Annex III.
3. US Department of State, *Trafficking in Persons Report*, 6.
4. Earthrights International Burma Project. *Entrenched: An Investigative Report on the Systematic Use of Forced Labor by the Burmese Army in a Rural Area* (June 2003), 28.

Chapter 4. Slavery Around the World

1. US Department of State, *Trafficking in Persons Report*, 14.
2. David T. Johnson, "Above the Law? Police Integrity in Japan," *Social Science Japan Journal* 6 (2003), 19-37.
3. US Department of State, *Trafficking in Persons Report*, 10.
4. Kevin Bales, *Disposable People: New Slavery in the Global Economy* (Berkeley, CA: University of California Press, 1999), 88.
5. British Broadcasting Corporation, "Slavery: Mauritania's Best Kept Secret," December 13, 2004. http://news.bbc.co.uk/2/hi/africa/4091579.stm.
6. Statement provided to Kevin Bales by Salma-mint Saloum, July 2003.
7. US Department of State, *Trafficking in Persons Report*, 12-13.
8. Ibid., 250

9. Ibid.

10. Reuters, "Sex Traffickers Target Women in War-torn Iraq," October 26, 2006. www.alertnet.org/thenews/newsdesk/ IRIN/38db2e39d044b5618c8e973059c18ca9.htm.

11. Namely, the Ansar Burney Trust and Anti-Slavery International.

12. US Department of State, *Trafficking in Persons Report*, 250-51.

13. Ibid., 5.

14. Ibid., 138.

15. Ibid.

16. Alberto Gonzales, "Prepared Remarks of Attorney General Alberto R. Gonzales," 2006 National Conference on Human Trafficking, New Orleans, LA, October 3, 2006. www.usdoj.gov/ag/speeches/2006/ag_speech_061003.html.

17. Free the Slaves and UC Berkeley, *Hidden Slaves: Forced Labor in the United States* (September 2004), 10.

18. Ibid., 14.

Chapter 5. Slavery and Globalization

1. Martin Albrow, *The Global Age* (London: Polity Press, 1996), 88.

2 Kevin Bales, *Disposable People*, 38.

3. CNN, "Study: Spam Costs Businesses $13 Billion," January 5, 2003. www.cnn.com/2003/TECH/biztech/01/03/spam.costs.ap/.

4. International Labor Office, "Fact Sheet on Combatting Forced Labour" (2005), 3.

5. US Department of Agriculture, "A Citizen's Guide to Food Recovery." www.usda.gov/news/pubs/gleaning/two.htm.

6. See for example, "Dying for your dinner," Environmental Justice Foundation, accessed at http://www.csrwire.com/ PressRelease.php?id=1932; and Report No. 32 on Forced

Labor in Burma, International Labor Organization, accessed at http://burmalibrary.org/reg.burma/archives/199809/msg00281.html.

Chapter 6. Controversies and Problems

1. Clara Jeffrey, "Who Gives a $%&t?" *Mother Jones* (December/January 2006). www.motherjones.com/news/exhibit/2005/12/exhibit.html.
2. Desmond Tutu, *No Future Without Forgiveness* (London: Rider 1999), 31.

Chapter 7. How We Will End Slavery

1. This is the Sankalp organization that works in Uttar Pradesh in partnership with the American anti-slavery organization Free the Slaves.
2. This work is being done by APPLE, a partner of Free the Slaves, which works along Ghana's Lake Volta.

For Further Information

ANTI-SLAVERY ORGANIZATIONS

Free the Slaves
PO Box 34727
Washington, DC 20005 USA
Phone: (202) 638-1865
Fax: (202) 638-0599
Email: info@freetheslaves.net
Website: www.freetheslaves.net

Free the Slaves is a nonprofit organization dedicated to ending slavery around the world. It is the main anti-slavery organization in the US with a global focus. Free the Slaves works with partner organizations to address slavery at a local level, raises awareness of the issue, promotes businesses and goods that do not have ties to slave labor, educates government officials about slavery, and conducts research on contemporary slavery.

If you want to take action against modern slavery, visit the Take Action section of the website. Here you will find sample articles for your newspaper or newsletter, suggestions on how to organize a film show, a fast, a spoken-word event, or a demonstration. Most activities have a checklist to keep you on track and make sure your event is successful.

Anti-Slavery International
Thomas Clarkson House
The Stableyard
Broomgrove Road
London SW9 9TL UK
Email: info@antislavery.org
Website: www.antislavery.org
Anti-Slavery International is the world's oldest human rights
organization and the European sister organization of Free the
Slaves. It has been operating continuously since 1787 and has
been at the forefront of every historical advance toward abolish-
ing slavery.

Canadian Aid for Southern Sudan
35 Bruce Street
London, Ontario
N6C 1G5
Phone: (519) 679-1429
Fax: (519) 439-4170
Email: cass.can@sympatico.ca
Website: www.casscanada.net

Canadian Aid for Southern Sudan works against slavery in
Sudan and helps freed slaves to rebuild their lives. CASS works
with the Canadian government to help it respond to the needs
of slaves and freed slaves.

WEBSITES

Free the Slaves – www.freetheslaves.net
This is your first stop for information about modern slavery and current action against slavery around the world, and for lots of resources.

International Cocoa Initiative – www.cocoainitiative.org
The International Cocoa Initiative is a foundation that works in West Africa to take slave labor out of cocoa production. The website contains extensive information about how cocoa is produced, as well as profiles of cocoa-producing countries, stories from victims, and fact sheets.

National Underground Railroad Freedom Center
– www.freedomcenter.org

The National Underground Railroad Freedom Center opened in Cincinnati, Ohio, in September 2004. It chronicles the history of the Underground Railroad and the fight to free slaves in the US before 1865. The Freedom Stations on the website are an interactive learning area where you can do in-depth research using a very large database of photos and documents.

Office to Monitor and Combat Trafficking in Persons, US State Department – www.state.gov/g/tip

The US government's main anti-slavery agency is the Office to Monitor and Combat Trafficking in Persons. Their website provides an introduction to anti-trafficking work around the world. The office publishes an annual report on global human trafficking, describing the situation in almost every country.

Rugmark – www.rugmark.org

Rugmark is a global organization dedicated to taking child and slave labor out of carpet-making and to offering educational opportunities to children in India, Nepal, and Pakistan. The website has a wealth of information on child labor and the reha-bilitation of child workers. It explains the Rugmark certification process and lists shops that sell Rugmark rugs.

BOOKS

Bales, Kevin. *Disposable People: New Slavery in the Global Economy*. Berkeley, CA: University of California Press, 1999; revised edition 2005.

Bales, Kevin. *Understanding Global Slavery: A Reader*. Berkeley, CA: University of California Press, 2005.

Bales, Kevin. *Ending Slavery: How We Free Today's Slaves*. Berkeley, CA: University of California Press, 2007.

Cadet, Jean-Robert. *Restavec: From Haitian Slave Child to Middle-Class American, An Autobiography*. Austin, TX: University of Texas Press, 1998.

Ehrenreich, Barbara and Arlie Russel Hochschild. *Global Woman: Nannies, Maids, and Sex Workers in the New Economy*. New York: Henry Holt, 2002.

Hochschild, Adam. *Bury the Chains: Prophets, Slaves, and Rebels in the First Human Rights Crusade*. New York: Houghton Mifflin, 2005.

Hochschild, Adam. *King Leopold's Ghost: A Story of Greed, Terror, and Heroism in Colonial Africa*. New York: First Mariner Books, 1999.

Kielburger, Craig, with Kevin Major. *Free the Children: A Young Man Fights against Child Labor and Proves That Children Can Change the World*. New York: HarperCollins, 1998.

Kipiniak, Chris, et. al. *Nightcrawler*, vol. 2, 1-4, "Passion Play."
New York: Marvel Comics, February-May 2002.

Kuklin, Susan. *Iqbal Masih and the Crusaders against Child
Slavery*. New York: Henry Holt, 1998.

Lebreton, Binka. *Trapped: Modern-Day Slavery in the Brazilian
Amazon*. Bloomfield, CT: Kumarian Press, 2003.

Meltzer, Milton. *Slavery: A World History*. New York: Da Capo
Press, 1993.

Miers, Suzanne. *Slavery in the Twentieth Century: The Evolution
of a Global Problem*. Walnut Creek, CA: Alta Mira Press, 2003.

Nazer, Mende and Damien Lewis. *Slave: My True Story*. New
York: Public Affairs, 2003.

O'Byrne, Darren. *Human Rights: An Introduction*. Essex, UK:
Prentice Hall, 2003.

Springer, Jane. *Listen to Us: The World's Working Children*.
Toronto: Groundwood Books, 1997.

Stowe, Harriet Beecher. *Uncle Tom's Cabin*. New York:
HarperCollins, 1987.

FILMS

All these films may be viewed free online and/or purchased at the Free the Slaves website.

Dreams Die Hard – 30 minutes – a film on modern slavery in the US.

Freedom and Beyond – 20 minutes – a film about children liberated from slavery in India.

The Silent Revolution – 20 minutes – about a village of debt bondage slaves.

Slavery: A Global Investigation – 80 minutes – won the Emmy and Peabody awards.

Slavery 101 – 10 minutes.

Acknowledgments

We want to thank our editor at Groundwood, Jane Springer, and Rachel Cornell for her help in the editing process.

Becky: I would like to thank my family and friends for their support and understanding during the writing process. Dr. Richard Del Guidice deserves thanks for teaching me to think and write clearly, and I am grateful to Kevin for the opportunity to write this book.

Kevin: I want to thank Jolene Smith, our leader and director at Free the Slaves. I also want to thank two students, Abbey Steele and Dan Hammer. Through their sweat and sacrifice, they helped pull the organization up by its bootstraps. In India Supriya Awasthi has accomplished many things, including collecting some of the amazing stories of liberation that appear in this book.

Groundwood Books would like to thank Leon Grek for drawing the graphs, Sarah Quinn for proofreading, Deborah Viets for copyediting, and Gillian Watts for the index.

Index